D0088930

WITHDRAWN

Praise for

The Imperfect Marriage

"I love how Darryl and Tracy Strawberry share that true repentance was the first major step in the restoration of their marriage. *The Imperfect Marriage* gives hope to every couple struggling in their marriage and on the brink of divorce. A must-read!"

—Joni Lamb, vice president, Daystar Network

"*The Imperfect Marriage* is refreshingly honest as it lays out practical steps needed to pursue God's design for marriage. Using their own personal stories, our dear friends Darryl and Tracy Strawberry also skillfully impart hope to those ready to give up. I believe this book will be a catalyst toward the restoration of many marriages!"

—John Bevere, author, speaker, and cofounder of Messenger International

the IMPERFECT MARRIAGE

Help for Those Who Think It's Over

DARRYL *and* TRACY STRAWBERRY

with A. J. Gregory

HOWARD BOOKS
A DIVISION OF SIMON & SCHUSTER, INC.

New York   Nashville   London   Toronto   Sydney   New Delhi

Howard Books
A Division of Simon & Schuster, Inc.
1230 Avenue of the Americas
New York, NY 10020

Copyright © 2014 by Darryl Strawberry and Tracy Strawberry

Scripture quotations marked (NLT) are taken from the Holy Bible, New Living Translation, copyright © 1996, 2004, 2007. Used by permission of Tyndale House Publishers Inc., Carol Stream, Illinois 60188. All rights reserved.
Scripture quotations marked (NIV) are taken from THE HOLY BIBLE, NEW INTERNATIONAL VERSION®, NIV® Copyright © 1973, 1978, 1984, 2011 by Biblica, Inc.® Used by Permission of Biblica, Inc.® All rights reserved worldwide.
Scripture quotations marked (NASB) are taken from the New American Standard Bible. Copyright © 1960, 1962, 1963, 1968, 1971, 1972, 1973, 1975, 1977, 1995 by The Lockman Foundation, La Habra, Calif. All rights reserved. http://www.lockman.org.
Scripture quotations marked (NKJV) are taken from the New King James Version. Copyright © 1982 by Thomas Nelson, Inc. All rights reserved. Used by permission.
Scripture quotations marked (ESV) are taken from the Holy Bible, English Standard Version, copyright © 2001, 2007 by Crossway Bibles, a division of Good News Publishers. Used by permission. All rights reserved.
Scripture quotations marked (AMP) are from the Amplified Bible, Copyright © 1954, 1958, 1962, 1964, 1965, 1987 The Lockman Foundation. Used by permission.

All rights reserved, including the right to reproduce this book or portions thereof in any form whatsoever. For information address Howard Books Subsidiary Rights Department, 1230 Avenue of the Americas, New York, NY 10020.

To protect everyone's privacy, all names and identifying characteristics have been changed.

First Howard Books hardcover edition August 2014

HOWARD and colophon are trademarks of Simon & Schuster, Inc.

For information about special discounts for bulk purchases, please contact Simon & Schuster Special Sales at 1-866-506-1949 or business@simonandschuster.com.

The Simon & Schuster Speakers Bureau can bring authors to your live event. For more information or to book an event, contact the Simon & Schuster Speakers Bureau at 1-866-248-3049 or visit our website at www.simonspeakers.com.

Interior design Jaime Putorti
Jacket design by Jason Gabbert
Front jacket photo by Stephen Hershberger

Manufactured in the United States of America

10   9   8   7   6   5   4   3   2   1

Library of Congress Cataloging-in-Publication Data

Strawberry, Darryl.
  The imperfect marriage : help for those who think it's over / Darryl and Tracy Strawberry.
    pages cm
  1. Marriage. 2. Marriage—Religious aspects. I. Strawberry, Tracy. II. Title.
HQ734.S963 2014
  306.81—dc23
                                2013046845

ISBN 978-1-4767-3874-1
ISBN 978-1-4767-3876-5 (ebook)

For our children

Acknowledgments

Giving all Glory to our Lord, Jesus Christ, who is the author and finisher of our lives and faith.

To Our Amazing Children: You have fought your own battles while waiting for us to get it right. Your courage and strength are their own testimonies. The depth and degree of our love for all of you could never be measured. Although we are not perfect, this family has been through tremendous battles and we have come out victorious. We will continue to overcome! You children are the true heroes . . . ***we dedicate this book to you: Darryl, Jr. (DJ), Diamond, Alice, Omar, Jordan, Austin, Evan, Jade, and Jewel.***

To our amazing godparents, *Paul and Marjorie Leonard*, and amazing parents, *Gerald and Peggy Boulware*, who are the true examples of light and love. You have loved us through it all. We would have never made it without you. Words could never express our love for you.

Pastor Fidel and Theresa Gomez: You embraced us in the midst of our mess and changed our lives forever through your wisdom, love, and never-ending belief in us. We will love and cherish you always.

Pastor David Blunt: Through your devotion and commitment to teaching the uncompromised Word of God, we became free in the Word at Church on the Rock, St. Peters, Missouri. You have encouraged and believed in us from day one. With much love and our deepest gratitude.

To the Team who made this book a reality: Jennifer Gates, A. J. Gregory, Jonathan Merkh, Becky Nesbitt, and the entire Howard Books/Simon & Schuster Team! You are extraordinary people and it was such an honor and pleasure working with you all.

Contents

This book is not written for individuals in an abusive relationship. If you or your children are in danger, you need to seek safety. Call the authorities. Stay with family members or friends. Get help. If you don't have a place to go, call a local shelter or the National Domestic Violence Hotline (1-800-799-7233).

A Note from Darryl and Tracy

Our prayer is that we as a society rise up and take the covenant of "marriage" back. We know the battles our own children have had to bear and the great burden divorce brings upon society. We must turn it around. We must change.

You are worth it, our marriages are worth it and our children are certainly worth it.

Take Your Marriage Back. Embrace the journey.

—*Darryl & Tracy Strawberry*

Introduction

Marriage is a battlefield. Trust us, we know. Our marriage has suffered through—and survived—adultery, addiction, financial ruin, and the consequences of our own inner struggles.

It seemed doomed from the start.

When we met, each of us was twice divorced, unemployed, battling addiction, and fighting for sobriety. I (Darryl) came to the table with millions of dollars of debt, legal issues, and deep-rooted addictions to drugs and women.

In the course of my (Tracy's) addiction to drugs and alcohol, I voluntarily signed over custody of my children to prevent a nasty custody battle and was daily trying to find a reason to live.

We fell in love but were incapable of loving ourselves and each other in the way in which God designed us. After three tumultuous years of breaking up and making up, we finally married. Anyone in their right mind could have looked at this scenario and predicted ruin. It was almost comical that we thought we would make it.

To say the least, we weren't ready for marriage. We entered our union as two deeply broken individuals, consequently paving the way for more mistakes and deeper betrayals.

However, we finally wised up and let God in.

Though there were times we wanted to, we never gave up: on ourselves, on each other, and, more important, on our heavenly

Father. Through our surrender (and a lot of hard work), God orchestrated a miracle.

Today, we are blessed to have each other and enjoy a strong, healthy, fulfilling, and meaningful relationship. Is our marriage perfect? No. Of course not. We have our share of ups and downs, just like everyone else. We also have a strong desire to make our commitment last, just as God intended.

In recent years, we've had the extraordinary privilege of being appointed, by God, to build Strawberry Ministries. We speak to, and work with, thousands of individuals in our church, in our office, and at conferences across the country. Many are hurting, especially in their marriages. These people contact us daily, desperate for help. It doesn't take a rocket scientist or a handful of university studies to figure out that marriage today is in trouble.

Social media, chat rooms, Internet pornography, and many other cyber-sensations have taken hold of our relationships. Commitment doesn't seem to stand a chance against the power of infidelity, addiction, and selfish ambition. Many couples simply drift apart, falling into ruts and mindless routines. While struggling to meet the demands of each day, they lose their focus and feeling for each other. Spouses become more like roommates than lifelong partners and lovers.

How can couples move from a destructive, painful, or numb cycle of living into a marriage worth having? This book aims to answer that question.

Listen, we're not experts. We aren't licensed marriage counselors and don't claim to have all the answers. We are imperfect people with multiple broken marriages. We understand the dynamics of carrying baggage into a relationship. We know it isn't easy. We don't have a fairy-tale marriage, which doesn't exist anyway.

What we do have is a desire to get it right. A confidence that God desires marriage to last. We know that God is the ultimate author of change, healing, and restoration. He not only designs marriage, He redeems it.

You must first surrender yourself and the process to God. Then, you have to do the work. That's right, the work. While God will empower, lead, and direct you, you have to sort through your own issues.

God will do the healing, but you have to do the dealing.

Don't think for a minute your marriage is beyond repair. It's not too late for things to change for the better. It doesn't matter if this is your first marriage and you're new at this, or if it's your third and you're still flailing around, trying to figure it all out.

No matter how damaged your marriage, God can heal it.

No matter how loveless your marriage, God can reignite passion.

No matter how broken your marriage, God can bring about restoration.

In this book, we share our story, the struggles and the triumphs, so you can see how through the power of God and the process of change, He can transform a marriage from the inside out.

We offer a goal that you can achieve. We offer God's vision for marriage to give you hope.

Redemption.

Purpose.

Another chance.

A do-over.

You may not have a relationship as destructive or dysfunctional as ours was (thank goodness), but consider this: If we can make our marriage work, so can you! Whether your relationship is stale or falling apart at the seams, there is hope.

■

The Imperfect Marriage is divided into two parts:

Part 1: Me, will help you become more self-aware, see how your individual brokenness affects your marriage, deal with the brokenness, and understand the principles of trust and forgiveness.

Part 2: We, will explain God's design for marriage, demonstrate how to reshape your marriage, help you navigate the treacherous waters of temptation, and give you strategies for living well if your spouse has checked out.

These two sections will mirror the stages of our journey, from brokenness to healing to restoration, through God's love and guidance. Using our marriage story as a backdrop, we offer practical and revolutionary tools for common problems and obstacles.

The intimate details of our relationship are not the focus of this book, although we will invite you inside our vulnerable moments. We each have a story to tell. Ours isn't more or less important than yours. The lessons we learned are what really matter.

The purpose of this book is to help you revisit your story in order to recreate your marriage. We want you to dig deep and take an honest look at yourself

At the end of each chapter, you'll find some suggestions for reflection. Take the time and think about our questions. Meditate on them. Don't dismiss them as insignificant or unnecessary reading.

Write down your thoughts in the available space or in a separate journal or notebook. Think, really *think*, about what we ask, and pray for revelation. When you do this, God will speak to your heart.

The trenches of marriage are real. So is God's transforming power. Don't be misled. God will not fix your marriage overnight by waving a magic wand. Through His guidance and your participation, an unraveling marriage can be woven back together with an everlasting strength.

Are you ready to dig deep?

Are you ready to discover what God thinks about marriage?

Are you ready for God to change your heart?

Are you ready to fall in love again?

Are you ready to be inspired to transform your marriage into an enduring and vital relationship?

Let's get started.

www.strawberryministries.org

part one

ME

1

Lost at First Sight

I (Tracy) remember the first time I laid eyes on Darryl Strawberry.

When we met, we were deeply wounded souls leading destructive lives. Our first introduction was at a Narcotics Anonymous (NA) convention in 2003. NA is a program and support group for people who want to break free from the lifestyle of drug addiction and alcoholism. The problem was that we had not broken free. We were still fighting the demons of addiction and the accompanying consequences.

I wasn't (and still am not) a sports fan. I didn't know much about Darryl's baseball career. Frankly, I didn't care. What I saw was a gentle, broken man desperately searching for a spark of hope to keep on living. I recognized that look because I had lived in that place of pain and desperation.

At the time, I had been clean and sober for a year but still had a lot of healing to do. I was determined to get well, but struggled to define what that meant and how to get there.

Darryl was sitting in a high-backed chair in a corner, desperately trying to blend into the crowd. His thin, frail frame sank into that chair as if he were part of the upholstery. People swarmed all over him, captivated by his celebrity status, yet unable to see his hurting soul. I was struck by how graciously he greeted everyone and signed autographs with what little energy he had.

My heart was torn. I didn't know Darryl Strawberry, the celebrity athlete. I knew what I saw, a man with a tormented soul who had lost his identity. Oblivious to his hurt and need for space, the crowd just kept pulling and demanding more from him. It was a difficult scene to watch.

It wasn't long before our eyes met. A mutual friend introduced us. Our first conversation ran deep. Darryl and I were brutally honest with each other from the start. We were addicts who had blazed a trail of destruction through our lives.

Our dialogue flowed naturally and passionately. I could feel the chemistry. Darryl was easy to like and talk to. I felt comfortable sharing with him and wanted to know him better. But I wasn't interested in Darryl Strawberry, the ballplayer. Darryl Strawberry, the man, caught my heart.

By the time I (Darryl) met Tracy, I had partied hard for years, using cocaine, women, and alcohol to mask or numb my pain. In the process, I had destroyed almost everything in my path. My second marriage had just ended. My baseball career was over. I was drowning in legal problems. My money was almost gone. I was a train wreck. It seemed I had lived up to my father's words: "You're no good. You'll never amount to nothin'."

Life had left me bitter. Angry. Trying to find relief wherever I could. I've experienced the highs of championship victories and the lows of addiction. I had the power to get what I wanted, whenever I wanted. Women, drugs, you name it. But intertwined in the glamor of stardom was heartache. Emptiness. Pain. No amount of sex, money, or clothes; no number of houses, cars, or cocaine lines could ease it. So I fell. Hard.

My drinking and cocaine addictions led me to failed relationships, arrests, lawsuits, infidelities, league suspensions, and money problems. By the time I ended up at the NA convention, I had lost it all.

When I met Tracy, she stood out. It wasn't just because she was attractive. I had been surrounded by beautiful women for most of my life. They were a dime a dozen. Tracy was different. Kind. Compassionate. She paid no mind to Darryl the great baseball player. It almost seemed as though she didn't know who I was.

We talked for a while, sharing our stories, and listening intently. We poured our hearts out to each other. There were no secrets. Nothing to hide. Unlike me, Tracy was actually recovering. She was focused on staying clean and made that clear up front. I told her the truth—I was trying, but I was a long way from arriving. I even said, "Girl, you have no idea what you're getting yourself into."

We kindled a friendship that night and eventually started dating. I admired Tracy. She was a single working mom of three kids. The most beautiful part about her was that she was pursuing Jesus. She had just turned her life over to Christ. Even though she was battling with God and struggling to believe, she had a genuine commitment to growing spiritually. She was angry with God and had a difficult time believing that He could heal her heart and deliver her from deep-rooted addiction. Yet she chose to press through those feelings and embrace her faith. Tracy made the commitment to find out about Jesus for herself. She chose to follow Him and believe that He would reveal Himself to her along the way. She studied the Bible to get her own answers. She pursued Him with passion. I liked that. And, deep down inside, I wanted that.

Though I loved and looked up to Tracy, I didn't make life easy for her. I wanted to break free from the lifestyle of addiction. I wanted to get clean and be well. Sadly, the desire wasn't strong enough to make me do the work of change. I was still hanging out with the wrong people in the wrong places. I didn't know how to change, even though I knew that I needed to. Most of our dating consisted of her looking for and pulling me out of crack houses. We were supposedly in love, but incapable of truly loving one another.

Many people have their stories of love at first sight. For us, it was *lost* at first sight. By the time we met, we had lost relationships, our children, our marriages, our money, our will to live, and our connection with God. We were spiritually, physically, emotionally, and financially bankrupt.

Our hearts were all we had to offer each other, which would have been fine except that those hearts were a mess. They needed a lot of healing. An unhealed heart is a dangerous thing. It houses hurts, unforgiveness, bitterness, pain, and every other thing that strips its ability to function properly.

An unhealed heart cannot produce the proper character required to love someone the way that God intended. As much as we tried to love each other, we couldn't. Our addictions and the accumulation of unhealed wounds overrode our greatest intentions and efforts. We desperately needed a do-over before we even said "I do."

TIME FOR A DO-OVER

Think about the first time you met your spouse.

Where were you? What did you say? Were you nervous? Excited? Hopeful? Was it a chance meeting? A blind date? What drew you to your husband or wife? Indescribable chemistry? Physical attraction? What made you want to see him or her again? His eyes? Her smile? His muscles? Her outfit?

Think about your dating relationship. Was it fun and natural? Drama filled? Loving and engaging? Maybe you and your spouse were two stable and emotionally whole people pursuing a healthy and growing relationship.

Perhaps your courtship was far from that.

We had a relationship that was far from healthy. Our life together was combustive from the words "hello" to the words "I do," which would lead into words like "I don't" and "I'm done."

How does an "I do" turn into an "I'm done"? And how do you turn "I'm done" into a reformed "I do"?

Many times the "I dos" need a do-over. Not with another person, but with your current spouse.

One of the most amazing things about God is that He gives us a do-over the very minute we ask for one. Whatever the state of your marriage, you can begin again.

BLIND LOVE

When I (Tracy) met Darryl, I was searching for more. I was drowning in the aftermath of addiction to drugs and alcohol. The most heartbreaking consequence of my lifestyle had led to my ultimate nightmare: surrendering custody of my three beautiful children.

I had cleaned up my act on the outside but was empty inside. I couldn't find what I was looking for in meetings, programs, or the NA convention. I was strong. I was determined. I was focused. Sobriety alone wasn't the answer I sought. Something was still missing.

Have you ever been there? Wanting so much more but unsure of what exactly that is? Wanting to get to a better place but not knowing how to get there? You follow what seems to be the perfect GPS, the desires of your heart, only to find yourself right back where you started. The same old routine. The same old results.

Darryl and I desperately desired more. We wanted a new routine, a new way of living, a new outcome. We especially wanted a do-over in life and in relationships.

We fell in love. Fast and hard. Oh, that emotional GPS. When the alarms of physical attraction go off, it's easy to lose your breath and your footing. Desire bypasses reason, logic, or calculated intention. It's what many call *love at first sight*.

You are bewitched by beauty, captivated by strength. You are so enamored of a person that you can't see straight. You can barely eat. Your mind is consumed by thoughts of him or her. The butterflies in your stomach distract you from everyday life. Maybe that's how you felt when you met your spouse.

The kind of love that sees only what it wants to see is blind, a mere shadow of love that is fully informed.

Blind love falls in love with the potential of a person, not the nitty-gritty truth of who they really are.

Blind love tolerates deceptions that can very easily become your adopted truth, leading you right back into another unhealthy relationship.

Blind love tells you, "It will be different this time."

That's what I (Tracy) thought. I kept the blinders on and allowed myself to be drawn into another toxic relationship.

THE MISSING LINK—GODLY LOVE

God wired us to love and be loved. No one can escape the need for it. Love is as essential to living as oxygen.

The problem is that love the way God created it to be has been distorted by sin. Most times this four-letter word is defined by human desire instead of God's design. We chase after it according to the world's standards—love is connected to feeling good, looking good, getting something out of it, and other superficial ideals.

True love finds its purpose and fulfills itself within relationships that operate according to God's ways, and His ways only. First John 4:8 tells us, "But anyone who does not love does not know God, for God is love" (NLT). We can't love apart from God because God is love. He is the missing link in broken lives and broken marriages.

No one can claim to love God without knowing and loving Jesus. And to love Jesus is to obey Him. He said it Himself, "Those who accept my commandments and obey them are the ones who love me. And because they love me, my Father will love them. And I will love them and reveal myself to each of them" (John 14:21 NLT).

Love is grounded in God and evidenced through following Jesus. It requires a commitment to following God's ways. When we started dating, we didn't know what all that meant. We didn't approach life with anyone in mind but ourselves.

I (Darryl) was saved, but I wasn't living out godly principles. I had fallen away from God. Sure, I knew about Him. I had even given my life to Him at one point and went to church and read my Bible. But I was caught up in my old ways of thinking, being, and acting. I was spiritually and emotionally stumbling in the dark. Losing everything made me feel ashamed. Lost. Hopeless. And guilty.

By the time I (Tracy) hit rock bottom, I didn't want to hear about God, let alone walk in His ways. I had lived so carelessly, made so many mistakes, and hurt so many people that I couldn't even face God.

How do you repair, restore, and live right after so many years of destructive living? How could Darryl and I ever have a successful life full of promise, peace, and purpose?

These questions haunted me and kept me away from God for a long time. I didn't feel worthy of His time or His love. I didn't think God would even want to hear from a woman like me. I didn't believe God wanted to love, forgive, heal, and transform me. I didn't even believe He could.

Maybe you feel the same way. Do you question God's love, power, and grace because you messed up?

Maybe you cheated on your spouse.

Maybe you are holding on to past failures.

Maybe you've been married multiple times and your current marriage is on the verge of ending.

Let's get one thing straight—there is nothing, and we

mean *nothing*, that can separate you from the love of God. Not your past. Not your failures. Not your hang-ups. Not your slipups.

> *Neither death nor life, neither angels nor demons, neither the present nor the future, nor any powers, neither height nor depth, nor anything else in all creation, will be able to separate us from the love of God that is in Christ Jesus our Lord.*
>
> *Romans 8:38–39 (NIV)*

God loves you. And He is not only capable of redeeming and restoring you and your marriage, He longs to! He wants you to experience His love, true love, in your heart and with your spouse.

FINDING THE WAY BACK TO LOVE

Love in today's world needs to be redefined. The desire to love and be loved hasn't changed, but the way people do it must be transformed.

Restoration within a marriage is a process. It takes time. It takes more than just inspiration, it requires direction and application. You may wonder: *What does a successful marriage look like? How is it accomplished? How can I achieve restoration? What do healing and growth look and feel like?*

We can assure you it takes more than just a few prayers and shouts of praise. You have to go through to get to. Invest your time in self-evaluation and reflection through the eyes of

Christ, filtered through His grace. This will require revisiting your past, contemplating your actions, and challenging your perspectives.

It's important to note that the purpose of reflecting on your history is not to make you feel bad. You don't do this to wallow in your pain or embrace your shame. We urge you to look back so you can shed light on the dark parts, uncover truths, and use that knowledge to build your future.

Look back to move forward!

Make no mistake. The journey of restoration is hard. It hurts, and it takes work. You'll need to put in the effort, take purposeful action, and have patience. But trust us on this one: The journey is well worth it.

We started in a place of brokenness, but through the grace and guidance of God have made our way out. You can too.

Put on the proper mind-set and suit up for battle. Not with your spouse, but with the enemy who stands in your way. You and your spouse are going to win this fight. God is able. He will enable you. God is all powerful. He will give you the power you need for restoration.

We've heard it said that people will change when the pain of staying the same becomes greater than the pain of change (making different choices). Within the process of change there is hope. You can rest assured that every difficult step of change produces a positive result that will lead you and your spouse into freedom.

GOD IS ON YOUR SIDE

It is not God's desire for you to live within a broken marriage. It is His deepest desire to heal you, teach you, change you, and transform your marriage. He can and will empower you and your spouse to turn things around, but only if you let Him and only if you do your part.

God is a gentleman. He will not barge into your life or work against your free will. He is a loving God who desires us to come to Him willingly. Think about that. Isn't that the way you want your spouse to come to you? Willingly?

Will you give your heavenly Father permission to guide your journey? Will you allow the Holy Spirit to invade every area of your life? Your marriage will not be restored in your own strength, will, or power. The power must come from God through the Holy Spirit in you.

What is your spiritual condition right now? Have you turned your life over to God? Are you right with Him? Does the Holy Spirit live in you? Maybe you have fallen away or have taken your eyes off God because of the weight and pressure of your struggling marriage.

We want to encourage you to take your burden, your sin, and your shame to Jesus and allow Him to bury it, forgive it, and cleanse every part of you from the inside out. Let God raise you up through the power of His resurrection. The very same power that raised Christ from the dead will become alive in you. It will revive, strengthen, and empower you.

You can die to your old self, your old life, and all that is hindering God's best in your life and the life and love of your marriage. Forgiveness, cleansing, healing, and newness of life begin at the foot of the cross.

God has already established the greatness of your life and your marriage, and He will bring it about. Sure, you will have to do the work, but the work is not yours to accomplish. You will do it only through the power of the Holy Spirit and your faith in Jesus Christ.

If you feel God speaking to your heart right now, spend a few minutes in prayer. Get your heart right with Him. Ask Him to forgive you. Ask Him to help you. Ask the Holy Spirit to enter your heart and open your spiritual eyes. Ask God to prepare you for this amazing journey, which you have already started. Ask Him to speak to you as you read this book and work through our questions.

Commit this process of restoration to your heavenly Father. And thank Him in advance for changing your heart and bringing your marriage to the place of greatness to which He has called you.

■

God's greatest desire is to restore us and our marriages back to Him. However, the journey begins with us as individuals. Before He can transform your relationship with your husband or wife, you have to allow Him to deal with you on the inside.

It's time to change your mind-set. It's time to define marriage through God's eyes. It's time to get rid of unrealistic expectations and set your eyes and hearts on what God says. Only when you change the way you think about marriage will your marriage begin to change.

SOMETHING TO THINK ABOUT

At the beginning of this chapter, you took some time to reflect on first meeting your spouse. Now, we want you to focus on the state of your heart at that time.

What was your spiritual life like?

Where were you emotionally?

What defined you?

How did you define love?

2

God's Vision of Love

We had plenty of false expectations and ideas of marriage that worked against us right from the start. None of them had anything to do with what God says.

I (Darryl) had no idea what a loving marriage looked like. I didn't think it was even possible. I was raised as a product of an abusive relationship. I understood violence and dysfunction. Happy marriages were something I saw in movies, not real life.

I was twenty-two when I married for the first time. My career as a ballplayer was taking off, but I had the maturity level of a kid. My girlfriend was pregnant and I believed that the right thing to do was to marry her. I loved her, but I wasn't ready. I didn't think about our compatibility or our future. I didn't consider what a commitment really meant. I just did it. I said "I do."

A split second later, I was saying, "I don't." I didn't have the will to say *no* to all the beautiful women who threw themselves at me at home or on the road. I didn't have the will to say no to the drinking or to the drugs, either. I don't think I really wanted to. Our marriage eventually crumbled.

The second time around was pretty much a repeat. My wife couldn't stomach the womanizing, drinking, and drugging and filed for divorce. Who could blame her? I was a mess. Our marriage ended on a sour note.

When Tracy and I married, I had no expectations. That's right. None. Zero. Nada. She was an amazing woman and I loved her, so I figured I'd just marry her. Kinda like I did with my ex-wives. Seemed like a good idea at the time.

We knew we loved each other. I was crazy. Tracy was crazy. Well, she was probably crazy because I drove her crazy. I wasn't entirely confident the marriage would last, but I hoped for the best. I guess a big part of me was apathetic about the sanctity of marriage. Getting married was something that I just did.

The biggest advantage in our relationship was that we both had the desire to seek Jesus. But while we loved God, we hadn't centered ourselves in Him. We didn't have the proper understanding of marriage as He saw it.

I (Tracy) came from a structured household led by loving parents. My mom and dad never fought, at least not in front of us kids. They were always cordial and polite to one another. They handled conflict between the two of them privately. They respected each other, and it showed in the absence of harsh words and thoughtless accusations. Marriage seemed so easy.

While I am grateful to have experienced such a stable environment, it formed in me a mind-set that marriage didn't require much work. I assumed it just happened. Boy, was I wrong.

All my life I held on to the dream of the fairy-tale marriage. My husband would be attractive, successful, and fun. We would fall in love, have lucrative careers, live in a big house, make a few babies, and go on vacations. The man of my dreams would naturally be mindful of me, faithful, and caring. He would love being with me all the time. No other woman would ever catch his eye or his heart.

When I started dating, I was drawn to men by physical attraction and how much excitement and adventure they offered. I expected all the other stuff to somehow fall into place. However, life can quickly destroy love when you are not equipped with godly wisdom, purpose, and a realistic approach.

I was lost in the fairy tale, in love with the idea and feelings of romantic love. I had a very unrealistic view of marriage and my partners. That's why my marriages didn't work out. I didn't realize success would require working hard and being God centered

God's meaning of love completely contradicted my definition of the word. Mine was based on my opinions, desires, and fantastic ideas. I didn't know God had a detailed plan and purpose for marriage. I had no idea that character, not attraction or romance, would be the defining element of success or failure within a marriage. As a result, I did not do what I needed to do to make my unions pure and right. I rolled the dice—twice—and lost.

DREAMS OF MARRIAGE

"He/she is my soul mate and completes me."

"A great marriage just happens."

"Love is enough and will conquer all our problems."

"My husband/wife will change once we get married."

These are just a few of the more common misconceptions people have about marriage. Unfortunately, they don't carry much weight.

When tension builds, the following comments tend to become the reality. You may say things to your spouse like,

"What's your problem?"

"You're supposed to love me just the way I am."

"This never bothered you before."

"I don't know who you are any more."

"This isn't what I signed up for!"

Sound familiar?

Everyone creates an idea of what marriage should be like, how a mate should perform, and who he or she should become. Usually it's a wistful, unrealistic imagining of being taken care of, cherished, and fulfilled by a spouse. After all, marriage is about living happily ever after.

Right?

Let's paint that picture.

I just know how my husband will be. I know he will show up at my office with a dozen beautiful roses delivered to my desk for all to see just how much he loves me. I will arrive home and he will take me out to dinner, not expecting me to cook after how hard I've worked all day. After we come home, I will pop my hair in a ponytail and slip into my baggy sweatpants, get comfy, and light a fire. He will listen to my every word (all 100,000 of them) and have such compassion for what I have gone through today as he listens so contently. After a long day, I will lay gently on my Prince Charming's chest, which is just like the rest of his buff, strong body, and we will snuggle and fall asleep in each other's arms. Oh, what a wonderful life this will be.

I just know how my wife will be. She will not be one of those women who come home from work and throw on her baggy sweatpants and pull her hair back into a ponytail. She will meet me at the front door in the hottest lingerie my mind could imagine, presenting my home-cooked three-course meal. She'll shower me with respect and appreciation for working so hard all day and taking care of this household. She will lead me into the bedroom . . . and let's just say I will eat my home-cooked meal later. After I devour that three-course meal she cooked just for me, she will massage my feet and I will fall asleep while watching Monday Night Football. *She will gently cover me, kiss my cheek, and softly say, "Good night, baby." Oh, what a wonderful life this will be.*

Lord Jesus, help us. This is a comical depiction of just how differently men and women think and respond. It illustrates how quickly unrealistic expectations can extinguish these fairytale hopes. Men and women are two separate beings who operate differently but are expected to become one and walk in agreement. A husband and wife are to agree even though they typically think contrarily to one another. *What's this?* you may think. *Am I supposed to meet the needs of my mate through a natural response that is not built into my nature? What's important to my spouse doesn't seem to be that important to me anymore. What's the big deal? I don't get it.*

Think back. Why did you get married? Was it because your wife was the perfect accessory to your life? Was it because your husband had a great job and would give you the kind of material life you never had? Was it because the chemistry was explosive? Was it because you were supposedly in love? Was it because it was the right thing to do after dating a long time?

Did your perspective of marriage include your dreams and desires or God's design? Did your definition of love embrace

God's vision of love? Do you even have a clue what we're talking about?

In today's world, it's dangerous to marry without proper direction. False ideas and fantasies about marriage set us up for failure because we are not prepared for the reality.

Do you know that a marriage license is the only license you can get without preparation and without passing a test? Think about that for a moment.

Before you can get a driver's license, you have to acquire a learner's permit. To do that, you must take a vision test, pass a written test, and spend a certain number of hours behind the wheel with an experienced driver. Then, to get your driver's license, you have to pass still more tests. The entire process can take six months to a year.

We train for ten plus years to enter high school. Four more years to graduate. And more years of schooling, classes, and tests in college and grad school to prepare for careers, vocations, and jobs.

Zero training for marriage required.

Zero tests.

Zero required credits.

Zero continuing education.

All you have to do is walk down to your town hall, produce identification, sign on the dotted line, and boom! You're qualified in the eyes of the state to be married.

A piece of government paper doesn't equip you for what's to come. It doesn't teach you that you need more than romantic notions to pay the bills. It doesn't prepare you for what happens when lust wears off and fiery nights are filled up with rambunctious toddlers and crying babies. It doesn't coach you how to hold it together when everything is falling apart.

We are an unprepared people entering into a sacred and eternal promise before God. Marriage has a distinct purpose. It is one of the most holy and challenging callings, and it shoulders a level of responsibility all its own.

Here's what we need to learn about marriage. It's a selfless union and lifelong covenant. It's a call to commitment, even though feelings may change or fluctuate. It's a relationship that warrants maturity, wisdom, submission, and common sense. Most importantly, it's a union that must be centered in God and His design. He will hold us accountable to our vows.

AND GOD SAID . . .

We want you to forget about your ideas, expectations, and illusions about marriage. We want you to create a new belief, a new way of thinking based on what God says in His Word.

Welcome to the beginning of your do-over.

The apostle Paul wrote, "Don't copy the behavior and customs of this world, but let God transform you into a new person by changing the way you think. Then you will learn to know God's will for you, which is good and pleasing and perfect" (Romans 12:2 NLT).

In other words, don't listen to what the world (society) says. Don't follow their ideas of love or marriage. "Listen to what I, the Lord, say."

The Bible offers us a specific blueprint for marriage, which we'll get to in part 2. Before we examine His plans, we need to talk about His intentions.

God's primary purpose is to shape Christlike character within us (see Romans 8:29). Simply put, we are to help each other get to heaven and to bring others along with us. This means laying down ourselves and picking up the character of Christ. It means leaving the old behind and eagerly receiving the new. It means saying, "Lord, make me a new person, one who is more like you. Cultivate me into the person and spouse you created me to be so that I am able to love and to live for You."

Through marriage, God develops a husband and wife into two people who practice and prove His love. His love draws a couple closer to Him and to one another. A personal relationship with Jesus Christ is the key to the success within a marital relationship.

Love is carried out through character. Most people want the love but lack the proper character, which is what Galatians 5:22–23 refer to as *the fruit of the spirit*, or "love, joy, peace, patience, kindness, goodness, faithfulness, gentleness, and self-control." These characteristics make us capable of love. And they are also what transform us into the image of Christ.

Think about marriage and how these traits are necessary to maintain a loving and healthy relationship.

You will need love when the romance wears off.

You will need joy when difficulties arise or life seems dull or unsatisfying.

You will need to hold your peace when you have misunderstandings.

You will need patience when you want to lash out in anger.

You will need kindness when you are annoyed.

You will need gentleness and goodness when the harshness of life arises.

You will need faithfulness when you want to call it quits.

You will need self-control to overcome temptation.

These characteristics protect and sustain a marriage. They make it work. If you miss out on this overall design, you set yourselves up for romantic disillusionment and a life of anxiety and frustration. You will be guided by unrealistic expectations. Your needs will be impossible to meet.

If you embrace God's purpose and work within your relationship to produce these godly qualities, you will enter into a marriage of possibility. You will lay the groundwork for success. You will be positioned to usher purpose, peace, and passion into your relationship.

YOUR PERSPECTIVE OR GOD'S PURPOSE?

Remember the statements about marriage we shared earlier? Let's revisit these unrealistic ideas about marriage and shed light on them. Note the vast differences between our notions and God's truths.

"My spouse is my soul mate"

This is a variation on, "He completes *me*." "She fulfills *my* needs." "He is *my* one true love."

We can thank chick flicks, reality television, and sappy love songs for this myth.

Believing that a mate will fulfill or complete you is a very selfish perspective. It also places a lot of undue pressure on your spouse.

In no way are we saying that a couple shouldn't work together to achieve happiness. We simply want you to understand the importance of becoming God centered, not self centered.

God designed marriage to be a selfless union. It's not what your wife or husband can do for you; it's what you can do for him or her. With the proper perspective, you don't lose yourself, you gain another. You bring yourself in to help your spouse. You enter into marriage understanding that you are there to help equip each other to carry out God's plan for your lives.

Marriage is about serving one another. It's about developing Godly character as an individual. It's about serving and loving your partner as Christ did for you, mindful of you, not Himself. Sacrificially. Intentionally. (Ouch! That might sting.)

We believe that selfishness is the number-one reason for divorce. This selfishness stems from marrying without the proper knowledge of God's design for marriage and from self-centered, self-seeking ambitions.

Before you can even begin to be spouse minded, you need to become God minded. When you know God, love runs deeper than feelings. When you follow and allow Him to transform your life into His image, you become a better spouse. You are armed with what it takes to become, among other things, selfless, patient, thoughtful, peaceful, and respectful.

A great marriage just happens

What could possibly be so hard about love? The feeling is great. The passion is amazing. The romance is sweet. Sure! Until bills pile up. In-laws meddle. You lose your job. Your wife gets sick. Babies come. You get depressed. Your husband stops helping with the kids. You find you have different ideas and philosophies on household chores, raising children, and managing money. Romance becomes a memory and challenges become commonplace.

We like what Bible teacher Joe McGee once said: "The greatest marriage you will ever have is the one you build." Good marriages are not handed to us. They are built. They take work. They require sacrifice and selflessness. You have to learn how to respect one another, deal with differences in a healthy way, and walk through tough times together (because trust us, they will come).

Jesus talked about the importance of obeying His teachings. In other words, we have to put his commands into practice. Just as we have to do with God's vision for marriage.

Anyone who listens to my teaching and follows it is wise, like a person who builds a house on solid rock. Though the rain comes in torrents and the floodwaters rise and the winds beat against that house, it won't collapse because it is built on bedrock. But anyone who hears my teaching and doesn't obey it is foolish, like a person who builds a house on sand. When the rains and floods come and the winds beat against that house, it will collapse with a mighty crash.

Matthew 7:24–27 (NLT)

Love is enough

As we've established, the world's view of love is distorted and destructive. It sells itself as sex, pleasure, self-indulgence, and the means to meet your deepest wants and desires. It is the most misunderstood, misused, and improperly pursued thing in this world.

Love in this sense is not enough. A superficial understanding of a commitment principle cannot sustain a relationship for a lifetime.

But love as God designed it can. And that kind of love *is* enough.

> *Therefore be imitators of God, as beloved children; and walk in love, just as Christ also loved you and gave Himself up for us, an offering and a sacrifice to God as a fragrant aroma.*
>
> *Ephesians 5:1–2 (NASB.)*

God's love is rooted and grounded in faith. It anchors itself deeply in commitment and is stronger than feelings. It seeks and desires to fulfill the purpose of marriage. This kind of love can only be fulfilled through the plan, design, and direction of God. When godly love is achieved, the feelings of love will be there.

We like the way *The Message* Bible translation conveys the most popular Bible passage on love. These verses illustrate how love acts, walks, and talks. It is how love is carried out.

> *Love never gives up.*
> *Love cares more for others than for self.*
> *Love doesn't want what it doesn't have.*
> *Love doesn't strut,*
> *Doesn't have a swelled head,*
> *Doesn't force itself on others,*
> *Isn't always "me first,"*
> *Doesn't fly off the handle,*
> *Doesn't keep score of the sins of others,*
> *Doesn't revel when others grovel,*

Takes pleasure in the flowering of truth,
Puts up with anything,
Trusts God always,
Always looks for the best,
Never looks back,
But keeps going to the end.

(1 Corinthians 13:4–7)

If this type of love seems like a mighty mountain to climb, that's because it is. This popular text is often beautifully framed, exquisitely stenciled, and carefully displayed in living rooms everywhere. However, looking at it on a wall and doing it in a marriage are two entirely different things.

You can only love this way when you are grounded in God's foundational structure for marriage. As 1 John 4:8 tells us, we can only love if we know God because God is love.

My husband/wife will change

Many believe that an eternal pledge at the altar will change a spouse. After all, love is pretty powerful, right? But does it have the influence to completely modify someone's behavior, transform thinking, fix wayward ways, or remedy bad habits?

No.

However your wife or husband acted, thought, and treated you before you were married will likely remain the same afterward.

Be honest. Did you think that when you got married your spouse would

Stop cheating and become faithful?

Stop partying and become responsible?

Stop spending money and saving more?

Be less selfish and more attentive?

Live up to his or her potential?

Work as hard as you do to make this thing work?

Change . . . in some way, shape, or form?

Many marriages have been torn apart by toxic beliefs like these. The truth is, you cannot change your spouse. A home-cooked meal can't do it. An array of sexy lingerie can't do it. Money can't do it. Manipulation can't do it. What you can do, however, is model healthy behavior. Being an example exerts the proper influence.

God is the only one who can change people. And even He doesn't barge into our lives. People have to embrace the journey and make the choice to change. He will equip you with the right tools, but there is a condition: You must first submit to the process. Change only occurs when you make the choice and embrace His way of living. God can change your character when you follow His instructions and put His principles into action.

MAKE THE SHIFT

Maybe you entered marriage with the wrong expectations or improper understanding of God's perspective. Maybe you wonder if there is any hope for you and whether you can turn things around. Or maybe you and your spouse entered with God's design in mind but have lost your way.

There is hope and help for each and every one of us. God will meet you right where you are, in the midst of the storm or in the middle of the mess. Your love may be lost, but God's mission is for it to be found, restructured, rebuilt, and restored. If you both allow the power of Jesus Christ to enter into your marriage, and if you do your part, He will heal and renew every part of your relationship.

Restoration begins with the proper mind-set of marriage as defined by God. We have to define and establish who and what He wants us to become before we can take the proper steps.

We want you to revisit your attitude toward marriage. If it differs from God's plan, redefine your outlook. Pray and ask God to change not just your way of thinking, but your heart. This will change the way you talk to one another and treat each other.

When you view your marriage from a spiritual perspective and look at the bigger picture—beyond what your spouse can do for you—you will begin to grow. And that's when things can start to change.

Here are some steps to help you make that shift:

Make a commitment to view marriage through God's eyes, not the world's standards

I (Tracy) was influenced by society's views and standards of love. I thought love and romantic feelings were the same. I was immature and unrealistic. I was unprepared. I was weak in love. I gauged the success of love on my emotions, whether my needs were being met, and whether my fairytale expectations were becoming a reality.

Stop believing what Hollywood movies, *Sports Illustrated*, romance novels, the women at the hair salon, your buddies, or anyone or anything says about marriage (unless, of course, it aligns with the word of God).

Conform yourself to what God says.

Keep in mind that this takes time. It takes a while for the mind to catch up and overtake your old reality. It takes time to grasp truth. And it may not be natural for you. Our advice is to hang in there. Renew your mind by constantly reminding yourself of the truth.

Keep God first in your life

He is going to equip you to love. My (Tracy's) favorite Scripture verse about love is 1 John 4:8 (NIV): "Whoever does not love does not know God, because God is love." When I read this verse for the first time years ago, it arrested my attention. It explained why I was incapable of true love—I didn't know God.

When you know God, love runs deeper than feelings. When I make Him a daily priority, I am a better wife to Darryl. I am prepared to love him even through hard times. I am equipped to be selfless, patient, thoughtful, peaceful, and respectful.

This is the primary theme of this book. Life always comes back to Him. Neither you nor your spouse should be the center of your universe. That's God's place. Your spouse does not complete you. God does. And your wholeness in Him is what makes you the better half to your partner.

Abide in God

This is more than knowing God. It's about living for God. When you surrender to Him, you need to live for Him. Jesus said, "The truth will set you free" (John 8:32 NIV). Most people don't know the preceding verse. It includes a condition, which makes this popular saying possible.

In verse 31, Jesus said He will call you His disciple, or follower, if you abide in Him. Depending on the translation you read, *abide* means holding fast, living by, or being faithful to His teachings. Only when you do this will you know the truth and be set free.

People ache in marriages because they have expectations that can never be fulfilled. They are constantly disappointed, frustrated, and angry. The more you study the Bible, the more truth you know, the more you seek God in prayer, and the more knowledge you gain from wise teachings and books, the more freedom you will experience.

Once Darryl and I focused our eyes on God individually, we had a mind shift. We began to understand why our expectations were off base, and we changed course. Instead of being disconnected, we engaged our purpose in God. This happened because we took the time to pray and to actively seek truth.

Want a better marriage? Give God His rightful place in your life, then make a commitment to spend time with Him. And do yourself a favor: Don't just punch in a time card at church on Sundays. Spend quality time with Him every day. Don't watch the clock. And don't feel as though you have to pray for five hours a day. It's about spending personal time with Him.

Some of you have already made that commitment. Great! Keep at it. It's easy to get discouraged and leave God on the sidelines when you're going through a rough time, especially in marriage. But don't forget or marginalize His redemptive power.

God is able to restore your relationship. He is able to repair what has been broken. But He has to start with you, even if you are the one hurting from a betrayal or infidelity.

Understand that if nothing changes, nothing changes

If your marriage is on the rocks, if you don't like your wife, if you are upset with your husband, if you wonder why on earth you got married in the first place, realize that what you are doing is not working. Unless you pursue truth, your marriage will not improve. It will likely get worse.

Now, flip that phrase around. If something changes, then everything can begin to change! Embrace the change! You and your marriage are worth it!

SOMETHING TO THINK ABOUT

What were your expectations of marriage when you walked down the aisle? Were you caught up in romantic notions or the flurry of wedding planning?

How does your marriage today look different from the image you created in your mind? What is better? What are you hoping to improve? What needs to be changed?

Think about God's purpose for marriage. What are some truths that have challenged you? What are some areas that you need to work on? Where can you invite God in to change your mind-set and your heart?

3

The Heart of the Matter

About a year after I (Darryl) married Tracy, I got dressed one morning and stared long into the mirror. I was so tired of marriage at that point. I told God, "I'm sick of this. My wife is crazy! This relationship is crazy!"

In my heart, I heard God so clearly tell me, "No. Your wife isn't the problem. Nor is your marriage. You are." His words hit me like a sucker punch to my core. I'll never forget them.

So often, I pointed the finger at Tracy, calling out her failures, her flaws, her character defects. I wanted to fix her, when in fact I needed to fix myself. God had to purge me of my sin, my addictions, and my bad habits, behaviors, and attitudes before Tracy and I could work on our relationship.

My garbage wasn't Tracy's garbage. It was mine. And it was destroying my marriage.

I came into this marriage with a lot of wounds that needed healing. They stemmed from my core issues of distrust, unforgiveness, and fear. I didn't know how deep-rooted these toxic growths were, and how hurt I was on the inside.

I had trust issues. Because of my previous relationships and my experience with people who only wanted to know me for what I could offer them, I didn't trust anyone. I didn't trust God. I didn't even trust Tracy, though I knew in the bottom of my heart that she was a woman of integrity. I certainly didn't trust anyone to love me unconditionally.

My lack of trust surfaced in explosive fights with my wife. I was suspicious of everything she did. I didn't want to admit and deal with my baggage, so I focused on her.

Was she really going shopping?

What was she really doing with our money?

Who was she hanging out with when I was traveling?

I'd call her integrity into question and make false accusations.

However, Tracy wasn't the problem. She wasn't the source of my insecurities. I was. I was the one philandering. I was the one who wasn't keeping his word.

I also struggled with unforgiveness. I hadn't forgiven my father. I hadn't forgiven my ex-wives. I hadn't forgiven anyone who hurt me in the past. Because I held those people hostage in my heart, I couldn't be free myself. I couldn't move on. I couldn't pass *go* and experience healing.

Bitterness flooded my heart. It showed in how I treated Tracy. When we had a disagreement, my heart would run cold and I'd think, "Well, I don't need you. I can do everything by myself." I would reject her emotionally and sexually. I didn't want her to get deep into my soul or even touch me.

Then, there was the fear factor. I was always fearful of judgment. When you're a celebrity, you're an open target. It's probably the hardest aspect of the star life to deal with. Everyone's got an opinion (usually not a good one), and they can't wait to share it. I was so tired of reading negative things about me in the headlines, some of which weren't even true. The thing that hurt the most was hearing how I was a waste.

I was so afraid of public perception that when I started dating Tracy and, in the beginning of our marriage, I stopped going out. I got depressed and hid in the house. I would lie in bed telling Tracy, "Why won't God just let me die already?" I can still hear her response: "Oh, Darryl, you're never going to get off that easy."

When you hold on to unresolved issues, your marriage will remain stuck. You can't move forward. You become like the Israelites wandering around the wilderness.

One day, I took a long, hard look at myself in the mirror. I could no longer blame anyone for my problems. That day in front of the mirror I finally understood that the only way I was going to be free in my marriage was to finally deal with my insecurities, my scars, and my hang-ups. I had to let God in to do His work.

When you finally allow God to come into your heart and make things right, He performs spiritual surgery. He brings all the garbage out of your heart and fills the gap with faith and wholeness. He changes you from the inside out and transforms you into the man or woman He has called you to be. That personal transformation is the only thing that can restore a broken relationship.

That day, I began to seek God's help. It wasn't a one-time prayer, and I wasn't delivered in an instant. It took time. We don't get into our messes overnight, so it's going to take more than one prayer to get out of them.

I sought God persistently, praying, "I need you, God. Clean me. Purify me. Tear me down." I humbled myself. I dug deep into the word of God. I surrendered to the Holy Spirit. I sat still before God and listened, learning about myself and learning about Him.

As I studied the Bible, I realized I wasn't the only one who had issues. Great men like Abraham, Isaac, Jacob, and the apostle Peter were messed up, too! God showed me that they weren't very different from me. But they knew who God was and they wanted to become the men God created them to be.

I like to say that I became a real man the moment I humbled myself, picked up my cross, and started following Jesus. Before that time, I was just a man who had stuff. My heart was full of empty holes that I filled with houses, money, women, drugs, and clothes. When the material things were stripped away, the holes were still there.

Through my transformation, God poured His love into me. He filled me with goodness and brought me on the path of understanding. He gave me a spiritual perspective. He showed me how to love my wife.

When I finally positioned myself in the hands of the Great Physician, I found freedom. I was free to love. Free to understand. Free to live. Free to live with purpose. Free to enjoy my marriage.

God cannot fix your marriage until you let Him fix you. He cannot begin the work of reconciliation unless you reach deep into your heart and begin dealing with unresolved issues.

Everyone has issues. Some people deal with them before getting married; others, unfortunately, never do and consequently experience relational challenges. And, while life is an ongoing journey of growing and learning in God, there are certain core matters that need your attention if you hope to see change in yourself and in your marriage.

Every part of you influences this relationship—the good, the bad, the pretty, and the pretty ugly! If you want an outward change in your marriage, you are going to have to do the inside work.

Want a better *we*? Become a better *me*.

Friend, God is in the business of bringing growth. You can't do it on your own. Get out of the way and let Him be God. I know the process is painful. I went through it. I encourage you not to quit.

Hang in there.

Pray.

Keep seeking God in prayer.

Be still and listen to what the Spirit is saying.

Trust me; your mess can be turned into a message from God.

AN UNHEALED HEART IS DANGEROUS

"I love you with all my heart!"

You recite your vows in front of witnesses and seal your words with a kiss. You place your heart right into the hands of your wife or husband to cherish until death do you part. We believe most married couples misunderstand this notion of exchanging hearts.

The Bible says, "The human heart is the most deceitful of all things, and desperately wicked. Who really knows how bad it is?" (Jeremiah 17:9 NLT). What an eye-opening truth. You promise to give your spouse the most desperately wicked and deceitful of all things—your heart.

Yet the heart is very popular. People write songs about it, model jewelry after it, exchange cards about it. Couples offer it as a promise of undying love. Contemporary western culture embraces the romantic notions of the heart, and suggests it's responsible for our happiness and joy. Many submit to that deception.

There is a danger in conforming and adopting your thinking and beliefs to the ways of this world. The world leaves God out of the life picture. It makes us believe we can develop our own idea of marriage, how we think it should operate, and what we want to get out of it. It promotes the pursuit of happiness through self-satisfaction. It romances the reality right out of marriage. The world bases *I do* on personal wants, desires, and ideas, not on what God says.

The heart is the very core of our being. Most of us understand the physical importance of a healthy heart. If not cared for properly, this vital organ may become damaged. Environmental pollutants, harmful habits, and physical defects can cause internal injury. If left unaddressed or untreated, an unhealthy heart may even die.

What about the emotional component of the heart? The part that is responsible for developing character? *Character* is defined as "consistent behavior, moral nature, and makeup." It's formed by belief systems, personal experience, knowledge, and opinions, and is evidenced through behavior.

The emotional component of the heart can also get sick. It houses hurts from wounding experiences. It can grow in wickedness from the evils in this world. It can be damaged by unforgiveness and deceptive thinking. A sick, unhealed heart produces bad character.

Bad character brings forth many issues into a marriage. It creates a heaviness that no one can carry. It strips away the ability to love. A damaged heart cannot identify what is wrong and therefore lashes out in frustration, pain, and anger; usually toward the one you love most, your spouse.

An unhealed heart desperately searches for relief, happiness, wholeness, and healing in a person, place, or thing instead of through its Creator and Healer, Jesus Christ. It falls for the lie that falling in love is the cure; in reality, it damages the love you so desperately desire.

This is a natural problem that requires a spiritual solution. Only the gentle and adept hand of the Holy Spirit can conduct successful spiritual surgery. Only God's healing power can restore proper function to the heart.

WHAT IS THE CONDITION OF YOUR HEART?

By the time you marry, you have been shaped to some degree by life experiences. This can be a positive thing.

You may have learned to live life to the fullest and appreciate every moment through the way your parents modeled unconditional love and joy. You may handle your money wisely because of how a close relative responsibly managed finances and made profitable investments. You may have a close relationship with God because you were raised in a stable environment of faith.

Shaping can also have a negative effect, as it did in our case. Unresolved issues stemming from childhood, a traumatic experience, addictive tendencies, harsh-religious upbringing, hurts, hang-ups, and heartaches can cause damage to individuals and their most important relationships.

Being sexually assaulted as a child may bring about distrust in your marriage. A string of abusive relationships may cause you to fear and suspect your spouse. Past disappointments or betrayals may tempt you to build up internal walls to protect your true heart.

We encourage you to step outside your marriage and inside yourself.

Consider your internal struggles. Are you even aware of them? When was the last time you took your mind and attention off your spouse and your rocky marriage and took a good, long, hard look at yourself?

Take a moment to pause. Take a deep breath. Focus inward.

Do you struggle with unforgiveness? Anger? Mistrust? Pride? Identity or self-worth? Are you suspicious of people? Do you refuse to be vulnerable and constantly put up walls? Do you struggle to stay faithful?

Before you continue reading this chapter, ask God to excavate inner hurts that need to be healed in order to experience a breakthrough in your marriage. Give Him permission to examine, search, and renew your heart and mind.

Don't run from Him because you may be embarrassed or afraid to do this. Run toward Him. Open up your heart to Him.

We know this can be a frightening experience. It's not easy to cast the spotlight on your inner self. Self-examination may expose guilt, shame, or deep hurt. These feelings are normal and may cause you pain. They are not meant to hinder you, however, but to heal you. They are a wake-up call to return your heart to God and allow Him to do His great work within you.

God doesn't want you to continue living in brokenness. He sent His Son into the world to heal the brokenhearted and bind up their wounds (Psalm 147:3). Jesus came to earth to live and die for a purpose. That purpose is you.

Jesus didn't come to judge, condemn, or make your life miserable. He didn't come to point out your flaws or remind you how awful your marriage is. Jesus came to heal your bitterness. He came to heal your fears. He came to heal your anger. He came to heal your disappointment. He came to make all things new.

> *Anyone who belongs to Christ has become a new person.*
> *The old life is gone; a new life has begun!*
>
> *2 Corinthians 5:17 (NLT.)*

You are valuable. You owe it to yourself to step into this place with Jesus. Embrace your healing. Embrace the new you.

START THE WORK, BEGIN TO HEAL

When breakdowns occur in a marriage, it's easy to blame the other person.

It's his fault.
She's the one who cheated.
He spent all our hard-earned savings.
She stopped having sex with me.
He is never around.

She loves her career more than me.

He drinks too much.

Guess what? Your spouse is not your problem. Your husband is not your responsibility. Your wife is not your project to fix. God doesn't call you to point out and reconstruct your partner's character flaws. He does, however, call you to work on yourself.

It's important to understand that the Holy Spirit does not change the relationship. He changes the people who are in the relationship.

Embrace the fact that you have to look inward to get an outward result. When you are whole and healed on the inside, you are positioned to face your problems on the outside.

Change doesn't happen by chance. It happens by choice. Choose to dive into your core, surrender to God, and allow Him to reveal and heal the deepest, darkest hurts that are humanly impossible to reach.

Change also doesn't happen overnight. It takes time. How many years have you carried around unresolved guilt, shame, anger, resentment, and unforgiveness? How long have you struggled with low self-esteem, self-doubt, and fear? Sure, instantaneous inner healing can occur, but it's not the norm. Give yourself time. And give yourself some grace through the process.

The following five keys are what changed us from the inside out. They unlocked the door to freedom. This is how the spirit of God healed us and made us whole as individuals before He restored our marriage.

These keys are not going to turn you into a perfect person or give you a perfect marriage. These keys will, however, equip you to heal and keep your heart pure. Staying that way is a daily process that lasts a lifetime.

Along with practicing these five keys, you can seek additional wisdom and counsel from a pastor, counselor, psychologist, or mentor. You might want to read and study books about the particular areas in which you struggle. Ask God to reveal specific help He might want you to pursue to attain emotional wholeness.

KEY 1

Take ownership of your life and your actions through self-examination

You must take responsibility for your own life, for your own actions, for your own behavior. Own up to your flaws. You don't need to air out your dirty laundry to everyone, of course. But you do need to be honest with God and allow Him to show you the truth about the condition of your heart.

You may have been sexually molested as a child. Perhaps you are harboring unforgiveness. Maybe you are holding on to a traumatic memory. All these things may lie at the root of an anger problem, out-of-control emotions, a desire to drink, overeat, or compulsively shop. Whatever you don't allow God to conquer within you will continue to conquer you.

It's important to remember that no one is perfect. Digging deep to find the broken pieces of yourself does not mean you are a bad person. A screwup. A failure. Or that you'll never get it together. It just means that you are human. You are flawed. And you need God to make you whole.

King David was well aware of the need for self-examination. He wrote, "Search me, O God, and know my heart; Try me and know my anxious thoughts; And see if there be any hurtful way in me, And lead me in the everlasting way" (Psalm 139:23–24 NASB).

KEY 2

Place your life in the hands of the great Healer

Early in our marriage, I was haunted by the memory of being raped when I was a little girl. The deeply embedded and painful experience was particularly triggered when Darryl and I were being physically intimate. It wouldn't take much—sometimes just his touch, a particular word, or the simple presence of his body on mine.

The flashbacks were powerful and during lovemaking made me anxious and emotional. Many times I prayed for the act to be over with. This caused problems for us. Tension. It kept me from enjoying my husband in our marriage bed.

My resistance wasn't Darryl's fault. He never did anything wrong. He never mistreated me. He never forced me to do anything. The problem was that my heart housed the unhealed wound.

I couldn't shake the issue. I couldn't fix it on my own though I knew it needed to be worked out. It was causing my husband to feel undesired. Unwanted. Like a monster for even thinking of wanting to make love to his wife.

Something had to change.

I took this matter into my prayer closet with God and asked Him to heal me. The process began with forgiving my abuser by releasing him to God. I surrendered the memory and the mental and emotional aftermath to Him and thanked Him for healing me.

I wish I could say my prayer was a magical experience that instantly made me feel better and made my issue disappear. It didn't. But it was a first step that began an immediate work in my heart.

A key component in my healing was talking to Darryl about the rape. He listened with compassion and sincerity. We prayed together that day. My husband was patient, kind, and understanding as we both journeyed into this process together. He encouraged me through his words and his actions, and constantly affirmed me.

The change in me and in our sex life wasn't just physical. It was spiritual and emotional. Today, nothing hinders our marriage bed. I enjoy my husband and we celebrate each other. I am so grateful to know the Great Healer. He can do all things. He can restore all things. He can heal all things.

Bad things happen in this world. Really bad things that are not your responsibility and are beyond your control. You may have been sexually abused, physically assaulted, or emotionally battered by strangers or even those who were supposed to love and care for you.

We know how deep those wounds can bleed. And we stand with you in faith knowing that if you trust God to heal you, He will. No matter how scarred your heart is, He can restore what has been broken. Not only that, but He wants to. God desires you to be whole, to be well, to be healed.

You cannot heal yourself. Yes, you will have to do the work. You may need outside help from a therapist, pastor, or mentor. You will have to run away from temptation. You will have to say no. You will have to make the right choices. You will have to control your temper. You will have to change your mind-set. You will have to exercise patience.

You will have to do all those things, but Jesus Christ is the one who will reconstruct you from the inside out and secure your victory.

> *And I will give you a new heart, and I will put a new spirit in you. I will take out your stony, stubborn heart and give you a tender, responsive heart. And I will put my Spirit in you so that you will follow my decrees and be careful to obey my regulations.*
>
> Ezekiel 36:26–27(NLT)

Without God, you can only attempt to gain freedom. You cannot recreate yourself through your own will and power. That is a setup for failure. When you surrender to God and allow Him to transform you, your mind becomes renewed.

Your heart heals.

You are given a brand new life through the power of the Holy Spirit.

You can love better.

You can give more.

You can sacrifice without begrudging.

You can compromise without keeping tabs.

You may be a Christian and still deny God access to every part of your being, into the deep where you hurt the most. Don't miss out! Your heavenly Father wants the very best for you. He wants to give you an abundant life, a healed heart, a mind free of torment. He wants to make you well. He wants to make you whole.

God is the only one who can cleanse, heal, and restore. Ask Him to deliver you from the root of harmful memories or events, your bad choices, unhealthy actions, and damaging behaviors. Invite Him to correct and change you. Allow Him to transform your mind and put a new spirit in you.

KEY 3

Recognize and stop the cycle of sin

The apostle Paul wrote, "Oh, what a miserable person I am! Who will free me from this life that is dominated by sin and death? Thank God! The answer is in Jesus Christ our Lord. So you see how it is: In my mind I really want to obey God's law, but because of my sinful nature I am a slave to sin." (Romans 7:24–25 NLT).

Nobody likes to talk about sin. It's not a popular topic because it makes us feel guilty, judged, and ashamed. Some pastors talk about it too much. Others hardly mention the subject.

Sin is a big deal. It's the root of every divorce. It comes from living a life without God. Selfishness and unhealed hearts produce sin. If ignored, sin in a marriage will breed division, destruction, and defeat. Even divorce.

Before a couple can move forward, sin has to be addressed. And stopped. A path toward restoration cannot be forged if one or both people are not ready and willing to stop the cycle of sin and participate in the process of restoration.

Sometimes we think of sin as these big, bad behaviors that are easily recognized. Like theft, addiction, or adultery.

But what about the sin of selfishness?

Pride?

Speaking harsh words?

Being disrespectful?

Criticizing, pointing out flaws, and demanding perfection?

Making poor financial decisions?

Emotionally pushing your spouse away?

Chasing after self-centered pursuits?

Yup, that's right. Those are all sins. And they were all mine (Tracy's). They defined my struggle to be a healthy *me* in my marriage.

When Darryl and I married, I was full of fear. I had a critical spirit. I hoarded money. I continually pushed Darryl away and defined our relationship by my terms. I made it very clear that I was in control. Our *we* was very much all about *me*.

I had my share of failed relationships and had been a single mom for many years. I fought hard to become independent and there was no way that I would let anyone come in and mess that up. I had promised myself I would never depend on another man again. So, when Darryl showed up, I allowed him to love me, but only on my terms. And only as deeply as I would allow him.

I was always waiting and preparing for something to go wrong. Darryl was going to do something stupid and I would have to end the relationship. I was convinced when it did, I would be just fine. I'd be able to care for my children and me. Don't get me wrong, I loved Darryl, and I wanted to be in a relationship with him, I just never wanted to *need* him. I made sure he knew it, too. You know, just to keep him in check.

I asserted my independence and stood my ground by speaking to my husband with bold disrespect. I would discount his opinions and efforts to lead the relationship in order to maintain my position of control.

I controlled our budget and grilled Darryl on every penny that he spent. See, I worked hard for what was supposedly my money. I always felt like there was never enough and I was always behind. Though I allowed myself the liberty of spending, I didn't afford Darryl that same privilege. At least not without my permission.

I called the shots. There was no way I was going to surrender control or allow Darryl to take his rightful place as the head of our household. Looking out for me first and foremost was my way of feeling safe. Or so I thought.

The reality was that these patterns kept me in a vicious cycle of sin that created quarrels and fights and rocked the peace within our hearts and our household. They produced much unnecessary pain and frustration. It had to stop. I had to stop. I had to take ownership of my behavior and actions, place my life into the hands of the Great Healer, and stop the cycle of sin.

The first step to end the cycle of sin is to stop living by the world's standards and start living by God's principles. Turn away from what society tells you will make you safe, happy, whole, and in control. Submit to God.

Do not conform to the pattern of this world, but be transformed by the renewing of your mind. Then you will be able to test and approve what God's will is—his good, pleasing and perfect will.

Romans 12:2 (NIV)

Renewing your mind means exchanging your thoughts for God's thoughts. This is done by reading, studying, and meditating on God's word, the Bible.

When you change the way you think, you will change the way you live. You will want to start living life God's way, not your way.

KEY 4

Change your environment and influences

When you are conquering the cycle of sin and entering into the process of healing with Jesus Christ, be mindful of your environment, including who and what you allow into it.

Where do you need to stop going?

Who do you need to stop hanging out with?

Who will hinder your growth?

What places will cause you to trip and slip up?

What or who will negatively affect your wholeness?

> *Bad company corrupts good character.*
>
> *1 Corinthians 15:33 (NIV)*

If you insist on staying in "your ways" you will hinder God's healing power in your life. The cycle of sin doesn't stand a chance of being broken if you don't remove yourself from the sin or what led you to it. Revisit your priorities. Evaluate where and with whom you spend your time.

You may need to cut ties with the person with whom you

used to drink, party, or gossip. You may need to stop watching movies that trigger lust. You may need to stop going to happy hour with your coworkers. You may need to rethink your relationship with a friend who is trying to convince you to leave your wife.

It took me (Darryl) a long time to incorporate this principle into my life. I loved Jesus. I loved Tracy. However, I kept hanging out with the same people and in the same places that would cause me to mess up. How could I leave the partying lifestyle in the middle of a party? How could I stop falling into temptation if I kept putting myself in places where I'd be tempted?

Finally, I wised up. I had to admit that many of the friendships I had were really superficial, based on the common bond of partying. It was painful to admit, but some of those people didn't want me to get healthy. They weren't interested in my recovery. They didn't care about my desire to change my life and live for Christ. I also had to stop going to parties, events, and gatherings that were breeding grounds for trouble.

I maintain the same boundaries today. I travel frequently to New York City, my old stomping ground and playground, to make appearances or to speak. There are plenty of opportunities to go to after-parties and other functions. As a man who is committed to his marriage, I do not go. Nothing good will come from my attendance. So, I fulfill my original commitment and return to my hotel room.

I learned this lesson the hard way. If you choose to stay in an environment that will hinder your growth, you will never experience healing.

KEY 5

Develop your character . . . all the time

When your root issues begin to heal, you start the process of developing character, godly character.

Godly character comprises the characteristics and nature of Jesus Christ. It is the moral core that we ask the Holy Spirit to develop within us. He is the only one who can change your desires and behavior.

> *But the Holy Spirit produces this kind of fruit in our lives: love, joy, peace, patience, kindness, goodness, faithfulness, gentleness, and self-control.*
>
> *Galatians 5:22–23 (NLT)*

Notice it says that the Holy Spirit produces these characteristics within us. Our job is to practice them.

Godly character seeks the heart of God.

It is awakened and arrested by conviction.

It turns away from destruction, temptation, selfishness, and indulgence.

It desires to live right because it is right.

When we came together, we were full of character defects. Bad character will never act right. The only cure for bad character is to allow the Holy Spirit to transform you through His power into the character of Jesus Christ. He does it. You can't. You can strive to be good, moral, and ethical, but you will ultimately fall short. God is the only one who can transform the human heart and re-create your character.

One of my (Darryl's) favorite sayings is, "It's not important to be important." I say it all the time. In this society, everybody wants to be somebody. That's why everywhere you look there's a new reality TV show popping up out of nowhere about nothing. People are desperate for their fifteen minutes of fame and will do anything to get it. This world says it's important to care what others think, to flaunt achievements and possessions, and to define self-worth according to a questionable set of values.

Developing godly character is what really matters. I had to die to what the world thought of me, what the world wanted of me, and what the world demanded of me. I came into the understanding that I needed to be crucified with Christ (Galatians 2:20). It's not me who lives anymore, but Christ who lives in me.

I don't do whatever I want to do. I don't seek after the things I used to desire. That man is dead. I removed myself from living in the false reality of self-importance and stepped into Christ's character. I live according to God's principles.

I define good character in a marriage as no longer living for me, but living for my spouse and my children. I live so they may see the light that comes through me. This is something I work on every day. It's about doing the right thing, even when I don't feel like it.

■

The greatest gift that a couple can give themselves, their children, and their loved ones is the pursuit of godly character. The feelings of love wear off, but character will last forever.

So, how can you develop godly character? As usual, God says it best, giving clear instructions through His word in Galatians 5:13–26. We like reading this in *The Message*.

This is a lengthy passage, so hang in there. It's worth the read. And pay mind to our notes, which sum up portions of the text.

"It is absolutely clear that God has called you to a free life. Just make sure that you don't use this freedom as an excuse to do whatever you want to do and destroy your freedom. Rather, use your freedom to serve one another in love; that's how freedom grows." (verses 13–14)

In other words, no more excuses.

"For everything we know about God's Word is summed up in a single sentence: Love others as you love yourself. That's an act of true freedom. If you bite and ravage each other, watch out—in no time at all you will be annihilating each other, and where will your precious freedom be then?" (verse 15)

It's all about love.

"My counsel is this: Live freely, animated and motivated by God's Spirit. Then you won't feed the compulsions of selfishness. For there is a root of sinful self-interest in us that is at odds with a free spirit, just as the free spirit is incompatible with selfishness. These two ways of life are antithetical, so that you cannot live at times one way and at times another way according to how you feel on any given day. Why don't you choose to be led by the Spirit and so escape the erratic compulsions of a law-dominated existence?" (verses 16–18)

The battle between God's ways and my ways (the spirit and the flesh) is real.

"It is obvious what kind of life develops out of trying to get your own way all the time: repetitive, loveless, cheap sex; a stinking accumulation of mental and emotional garbage; frenzied and joyless grabs for happiness; trinket gods; magic-show religion; paranoid loneliness; cutthroat competition; all-consuming-yet-never-satisfied wants; a brutal temper; an impotence to love or be loved; divided homes and divided lives; small-minded and lopsided pursuits; the vicious habit of depersonalizing everyone into a rival; uncontrolled and uncontrollable addictions; ugly parodies of community. I could go on. This isn't the first time I have warned you, you know. If you use your freedom this way, you will not inherit God's kingdom." (verses 19–21)

Doing life your way leads to an unhealthy, corrupt, and unpleasant life, a life outside of the kingdom of God.

"But what happens when we live God's way? He brings gifts into our lives, much the same way that fruit appears in an orchard—things like affection for others, exuberance about life, serenity. We develop willingness to stick with things, a sense of compassion in the heart, and a conviction that a basic holiness permeates things and people. We find ourselves involved in loyal commitments, not needing to force our way in life, able to marshal and direct our energies wisely." (verses 22–23)

God's ways bring forth a life of blessing, peace, and wholeness.

"Legalism is helpless in bringing this about; it only gets in the way. Among those who belong to Christ, everything connected with getting our own way and mindlessly responding to what everyone else calls necessities is killed off for good—crucified." (verses 23-24)

We need to die to self and embrace Christ.

"Since this is the kind of life we have chosen, the life of the Spirit, let us make sure that we do not just hold it as an idea in our heads or a sentiment in our hearts, but work out its implications in every detail of our lives. That means we will not compare ourselves with each other as if one of us were better and another worse. We have far more interesting things to do with our lives. Each of us is an original." (verses 25–26)

Don't just think of God's ways as merely a good plan but a way of life. Put them into action. And don't worry about what anyone else should or should not be doing. Focus on yourself. Focus on living a life of abundance and wholeness that Jesus came to give you.

IT'S YOUR CALL

For years, we kept God out of our lives. We refused to seek after and live for Him. Because of this, we paid a terrible price. You don't have to make the same mistake.

Our relationship was not the problem. God was not the problem. Marriage was not the problem. We were the problem. The issues we carried with us as individuals were destroying us from the inside out.

The miracle of transformation began when we made the choice to focus inward. The power to change and heal was available to us, but we had to take the first step. There wasn't a particular feeling or event that led us to God. It was as simple as a choice.

Once we got serious with God and entered into a deep and personal relationship with Him, the process of healing within our hearts and then our relationship began to take place.

The power of choice lies in your hand. What you will do about the condition of your heart is your call. The way out of heartache, addiction, temptation, fear, and disappointment starts with a choice. The path toward healing, restoration, peace, love, joy, and greatness starts with a choice.

Your direction will change when you choose to follow God's directions.

So, what do you choose?

SOMETHING TO THINK ABOUT

When we asked you earlier to search inside yourself, did you do it? Did you spend a few minutes thinking about it? Or did you ignore our suggestion and quickly continue reading the rest of this chapter?

If you took the time to self-evaluate, great! Write down what you learned and pinpoint areas that need healing. If not, now is the time.

Think about the recurring fights you may have with your spouse. Where do you think these come from? A place of mistrust or insecurity perhaps? Think about the fears you have that negatively impact your relationship. Do they stem from a previous abusive relationship or a past heartbreak? Think about your control issues that continue to spark heated arguments with your husband or wife. What is the root of these issues?

Begin the healing process using the suggestions we offer in this book. Ask your spouse for forgiveness. Focus on becoming whole, instead of trying to fix your spouse or your marriage.

4

Free to Forgive

I sat on my bathroom floor, arms huddled around my knees as I rocked back and forth. Here I was, face-to-face with another admission of Darryl's adulterous affairs. Forgive him again? Really?

I cried so hard I could barely breathe. I carried an unbearable weight of anger and bitterness. I knew I couldn't hold on to those feelings forever. They didn't come only from my husband's infidelities. His betrayals revived my own past mistakes and the pains caused by others. My heart, and really my entire life, was entangled in offenses.

Yes, I was tormented by the memories of my husband's infidelities. But I was also hostile toward the man who raped me when I was a little girl. I was angry because of how my ex-husband disrespected and treated me. I grieved my past life as an addict, the loss of my children as a result, and all of the bad decisions and choices I had made during that time. I was an emotional mess.

That day in the bathroom, I came to the end of myself. Frankly, it was about time. As I cried out to God that afternoon, I finally turned over to Him all of the lying, cheating, and turmoil in my current marriage and all of the overpowering memories of the past.

That day marked a new beginning for me. It was a first step in a new direction.

At some point in every marriage, someone will offend, hurt, or outright betray the other. And, at some point, you will have to enter the potentially unchartered waters of forgiveness.

Forgiveness is a gateway into healing and freedom. It keeps our hearts and our relationships healthy and free from bitterness, anger, and resentment. And it's something we have to practice in life and in love.

This subject is so greatly misunderstood that we've devoted an entire chapter to it.

REVELATION

On the day I knelt and cried on the bathroom floor, I had been struggling with forgiveness for a while. I had begged and pleaded with God for the strength and grace to forgive my husband, certain people in my life, and myself. I read book after book about the process. I meditated for countless hours on scripture.

And, oh, I understood the spiritual implications of unforgiveness. My spirit would shout, "Do it immediately! If you don't, God won't forgive you!"

Of course I desperately wanted God's forgiveness. I knew I

could never experience freedom unless He forgave me. My intentions were in the right place. My motives were pure. I said "I forgive you" in my prayer times out loud over and over to those who offended, violated, and betrayed me. I even blessed them, too. I did the same thing with conviction over myself.

However, no matter how many times I repeated those words, no matter how many Scripture verses I memorized and recited, no matter how many books I read, no matter how many steps I followed, no matter how much advice I embraced, something was wrong. The war within me still raged.

At times, I would feel temporary relief, and peace would settle in my spirit. It felt like forgiveness was working. But the second I started thinking about that person, that offense, or that mistake, my emotions would erupt. Bitterness would flood my soul. Anger would consume me. I would be right back where I started, needing to forgive again. It was a vicious and emotionally exhausting cycle.

Have you ever felt this way?

Do you battle with unforgiveness?

Are you struggling to forgive your husband for an affair he had?

Are you unable to forgive the person who molested you?

Are you clinging to how badly your mom treated you?

Are you holding on to a twenty-year grudge?

Maybe you think you have forgiven but you still experience the emotions coming from being hurt, betrayed, abused, or lied to.

When I finally had enough of this sick and twisted rollercoaster ride, I had a candid conversation with the Holy Spirit. I got deep. I got honest. My prayer went something like this:

"I love you and I have given my life to you through your Son,

Jesus Christ. You demand, not ask, that we forgive immediately. It's a requirement to be forgiven by you (Matthew 6:14–15). You say in your Word that your grace is sufficient for me and that I can do all things through Christ who strengthens me (2 Corinthians 12:9, Philippians 4:13). I know the promise of freedom comes with forgiveness. But I'm not free. And I don't get it. I am obeying your Word. I have done all that you ask of me. So why, God? Why am I still bound to this pain, this anger, this bitterness, and this resentment?"

I quieted my spirit. And in my heart and mind, I heard the Holy Spirit's answers. Loud and clear.

"My dear child, you do not understand forgiveness. You do not understand in your heart the work of the cross accomplished by my Son. You are trying to forgive with your head and your human efforts. But this must come through your heart, through my Spirit within you. Forgiveness can never be accomplished through you. It is not your work. It is the work of my Son, Jesus!"

Wow!

Right then and there I asked God to forgive me. I verbally released my bitterness for the last time. I placed my heart in His hands and asked for the power of the Holy Spirit to saturate every part of my being with the work accomplished by Jesus Christ—forgiveness.

Instead of focusing on the faces, the betrayals, the offenses, the sins, the pain, the anger, and the bitterness, I turned my attention toward God. And I began, for the first time, to rest in Him.

Think about your relationship with God for a moment. Do you trust His Spirit, the Holy Spirit that lives within you? Do you know him?

It's vital to connect with the Spirit because you cannot forgive without Him. He is the Comforter, the Healer, and the Revealer of the things of God. He accomplishes restoration. He is the Spirit of God who lives inside of you when you give your life to Jesus, but He operates with power when you surrender totally to Him.

You may say, "But, Tracy, I already believe. I'm a Christian. And I know the Holy Spirit lives in me. But I can't do this. I can't stop thinking about what my wife or husband did."

I get it. I thought the same thing. What I didn't know, however, was that my bitterness was hindering the Spirit from doing His work in my heart. Ephesians 4:30 teaches us that we can grieve the Spirit and quench His work by the way we live. Here's the thing: Although I was trying to forgive, I was living in unrepentant bitterness. I was stuck. I was also trying to accomplish the work of forgiveness on my own. Scripture was merely words on a page to me. The Bible had no real meaning. Or power. Or depth. This combination quenched the power of the Spirit within me.

Once I stopped feeding and focusing on my bitterness and renewed my relationship with the Holy Spirit, everything changed. I stopped rehashing the times I was hurt. The times others had failed me. The times I missed the mark. I stopped reciting in my prayers the names of the people who hurt me. I stopped begging to feel relief and for my own forgiveness.

Instead, I sought the Spirit. I buried my heart and my mind in the Word of God. I repeated daily my prayerful commitment: "I surrender to you, Holy Spirit. Do what only you can do!" (Zechariah 4:6). I began to seek the true meaning of what Jesus accomplished on the cross. It was during this time that the Bible came alive to me. The revelation flowed. I was captivated by what I learned.

When you put your trust in the Lord and rely on the Holy Spirit, you change. You become transformed. You are overwhelmed by power and peace. Your relationship with God becomes mature and real. Your faith is strengthened. Circumstances may rock your world but not your faith. Your entire being is renewed.

Then, and only then, will the impossible become possible. What once held you hostage—the offenses, the heartache, the pain, the suffering, everything that stems from the poison of unforgiveness—will no longer overpower, influence, or have any control over you. Jesus said, "Humanly speaking, it is impossible. But with God everything is possible" (Matthew 19:26 NLT).

BACK TO THE BASICS

Forgiveness means more than saying or accepting two or three words. The simplest definition we like to use is *to release*.

To forgive means *to release* everything that is attached to the offense—the person, the situation, the emotions, the feelings, the aftermath—into the hands of God so that it will never again infect your heart.

We've learned to forgive *quickly*. As soon as you feel anger or bitterness coming on from a past offense, hit your knees. Pray. Release whatever or whomever is consuming your mind.

The prayer of forgiveness is done in faith, not through feelings. Don't get confused if your feelings don't line up with the principle. Sometimes feelings can mess up everything. In fact, they'll kick you right out of the process if you pay enough attention to them. Don't worry about whether you feel like forgiving. God will deal with that as you walk in obedience to His Word.

From now on, whenever you hear the word *forgive*, immediately think *release*. That's all you have to do. That's the work. That's your part. You turn it over to God, bless the person, and embrace your freedom in the Holy Spirit by focusing on Him. Wham, bam! That's it!

In the rest of this chapter we'll unpack the big ideas of forgiveness, but the overall premise is that *forgiveness is not your work*. Many people try to work on forgiving, but the real work of forgiveness was accomplished by Jesus Christ on the cross. Think about it. If you've been hurt by your spouse, have you ever said, "You broke my forgiveness?" Of course not! What do you say? "You broke my heart," or, "You broke my trust." Forgiveness is never broken, so it's not something that requires your work. You don't have to repair it or rebuild it. You don't need to work on forgiveness; you need to work on trust.

Many people give away trust freely and withhold forgiveness. This is the exact opposite of what God tells you to do. In His Word, He is plain about these two subjects. As you'll read later, there are numerous verses that tell you to forgive. And there are numerous verses that tell you to guard your heart and to prove yourself and others trustworthy. Trust and forgiveness are separate principles that need to be approached differently. Here's a quick summary. We'll talk more in chapter 5 about how to rebuild broken trust.

FORGIVENESS	TRUST
Not our work, but the work of Jesus. Displayed through His character and the work done on the cross.	Developed and displayed through our integrity, character, and ability.
Immediate. Never broken. Never needs to be rebuilt.	Gets broken. Takes time to become trustworthy, to trust others, and to rebuild trust.
A spiritual command. We do not get to choose who we forgive.	Optional. We choose who to trust, and we must choose wisely.
Not proven. No one gets to prove to us they are worthy of forgiveness.	Proven over time by consistent, right actions.
Forgiveness is released, not accomplished.	Trust is accomplished over time.
There are no degrees of forgiveness. It's all or nothing.	There are different degrees, levels, of trust. They will not all be the same.
Forgiveness is a step, not a journey. Must be released before healing can take place and trust rebuilt.	Trust is a journey. The cycle of sin must stop before healing and trust can begin.
Forgiveness is the operational system of cleansing and purifying the heart.	Trust is the foundational block of relationships. Relationships are built on trust or torn down when trust is broken.
Forgiveness is not our struggle, battle, or issue.	Trust becomes a battle, struggle, and issue when it's broken.
Forgiving is an act of embracing your faith, receiving all that Jesus died to give you. It is the beginning of freedom.	"Trust in the Lord with all your heart, And lean not on your own understanding; in all your ways acknowledge Him, and He shall direct your paths." (Proverbs 3:5–6 NKJV)

A SPIRITUAL REMEDY FOR
A SPIRITUAL PROBLEM

Forgiveness is the greatest expression of a Christian's faith. It's how one acknowledges the power, love, and work of the cross.

When you wholeheartedly forgive your spouse for having a one-night stand, you model the grace Jesus offers. When you extend mercy and don't beat your husband over the head with a past failure, you model the love Jesus came to give. When you allow God to heal you from your wife's betrayal instead of wallowing in bitterness, you model the work of the Holy Spirit.

God commands us to forgive. This is not up for negotiation. Colossians 3:13 tells us to "Forgive as the Lord forgave you" (NIV). Jesus said, "If your brother sins, rebuke him, and if he repents, forgive him. If he sins against you seven times in a day, and seven times comes back to you and says, 'I repent,' forgive him" (Luke 17:3-4 NIV).

You can forgive, but the act of forgiveness is not something you do. Jesus is the only one who can accomplish that work. His death made forgiveness possible. When you forgive someone, you release the offender and the offense to God so that He can accomplish the act.

True freedom is found in the cross. Not only is it representative of Jesus's death, it's also where sin, sickness, disease, our old way of life, and anything outside God died. When you repent (turn to God and away from sin) and believe Jesus died for you, you release the old. You put to death all the things that shame, haunt, hinder, or drag you down a destructive path.

And you take on a new nature. "The Spirit of God, who raised Jesus from the dead, lives in you. And just as God raised

Christ Jesus from the dead, he will give life to your mortal bodies by this same Spirit living within you" (Romans 8:11 NLT).

When you choose not to forgive yourself or others, you deny the power of the cross. When you deny the power of the cross, you deny the resurrection. When you do that, you deny the faith. You flat out deny Jesus Christ.

It's hard to release what hurts, even if you know it keeps you from the good life. The many misconceptions about forgiveness make release even more difficult. Let's clear up and settle some truths.

FORGIVENESS IS *NOT* . . .

- A feeling. You will usually never feel like forgiving someone who has harmed, hurt, or betrayed you.

- Magic. Everything doesn't suddenly become okay simply because you forgive. You have to step into the processes of healing and rebuilding trust.

- A pardon or a gesture that minimizes the severity and consequences of the offense.

- Necessarily a reconciliation. Just because you forgive someone doesn't mean that you give him or her the right to be in your life. In some cases, you may need to release the offense as well as the relationship. This is true of an abusive or toxic relationship. Through prayer and God's leading, you will know when to sever ties.

FORGIVENESS IS . . .

- Freedom! The release!

- The power that separates you from festering anger, rage, and resentment.

- A requirement for God's forgiveness of you. "But if you do not forgive others their sins, your Father will not forgive your sins" (Matthew 6:15 NIV).

- The operational system that cleanses the heart.

- Your entrance into healing and wholeness.

- A choice. (But there's too much at stake not to forgive.)

I THINK I'LL PASS ON THE FORGIVENESS STUFF

If you refuse to forgive, bitterness will eat away at your faith and rob you of the power, promises, and blessings that could be yours through faith in Jesus Christ. You will not heal or move forward in your life or in your marriage. You'll remain stuck. We like the saying we've heard many times, "Unforgiveness is like drinking poison and hoping that the other person dies."

A couple we counseled years ago powerfully illustrates this truth. We'll call them John and Jane. John had an addiction to online pornography, including explicit chat rooms. When Jane discovered John's infidelities, she confronted him.

John immediately and wholeheartedly turned away from the addiction. He was genuinely repentant before Jane and God. He sought professional help and was willing to do anything to restore their relationship. Jane wanted to work things out, too. They both committed to restore their relationship and rebuild trust.

There was only one problem. Jane refused to forgive John.

Every counseling session we had with this couple ended the same way. Jane would say, "I'm still working on trying to forgive John. But I can't believe he did this to me and our family! How will I ever trust him again?"

"First things first," we told her. "You cannot begin the process of healing or rebuilding trust if you withhold forgiveness." We explained over and over the true meaning of forgiveness and reiterated that neither of them would ever be able to heal or rebuild trust without it. Jane balked every time we mentioned the word *forgive*. She would list countless reasons why she couldn't . . . or wouldn't.

"I absolutely refuse to forgive John. I want him to pay and to feel what I am feeling. If I forgive him, it's just like giving him a free pass to do it all again—to do anything he wants for that matter. I'm going to have to work on forgiving John. I just can't do it yet. And, for right now, he's going to have to live with that!"

Live with it he did—for a while.

They continued to show up for sessions that would result in the same cycles. John would repeatedly ask Jane for forgiveness. Even though John's behavior consistently proved his repentance, Jane wouldn't have it.

Jane wouldn't have it. Nothing was good enough for her. She continued to bring up the betrayal and throw it in his face. John did everything she asked, but she refused to forgive.

No forgiveness? No release?

No release? No healing. No rebuilding of trust. No restoration. No relief.

This battle went on for three years. Finally, bitterness took root in Jane's heart, and the powerful emotion of anger kicked in. No one in the home was safe. Jane became physically ill, and even emotionally abusive, at times. She started to drink and party on the weekends. She felt she had the right to do these things, given John's betrayal. She made it clear time and time again that she was entitled. No one could tell her differently.

Eventually, Jane became severely depressed. She lay in bed for hours, was regularly late for work, and stopped engaging in her life. She became withdrawn and disconnected. The bitterness from her unforgiveness consumed her. John moved in with a family member, hoping that the space would help. It didn't.

One day, Jane came by our office for a visit, without John. She was distraught, desperate for a spark of hope. Darryl left me alone with her, and we hit our knees. I asked Jane if she was ready to receive her freedom and forgive John. She replied, "No." I got up and led her to the door. I didn't even say a word.

Jane looked at me with tears in her eyes. "Aren't you going to help me?" she begged. I told her that I am not the Healer. Only Jesus could do this work. I was simply someone who could lead her to Him.

"Your bitterness is killing you," I said. "The first step to your freedom is one prayer away. One prayer. That's it. You just have to release and believe in the power of the cross. Let the Spirit of God do the rest. He is willing. Are you?"

Jane fell into my arms and wept. I could sense a change of heart. "I am ready," she said. We got on our knees again and prayed. Together we sought the power of the Holy Spirit.

I encouraged Jane to pray from her heart and not quote some fancy, rehearsed words. I urged her to release John and herself into the arms of forgiveness. For forty minutes, she prayed and cried. It was a beautiful moment that I will never forget.

By the time Jane left our office, her entire demeanor had changed. She no longer felt depressed, angry, and resentful. She didn't look worn out and beaten up. She walked out the door strengthened, full of confidence and hope. The transformation was an absolute miracle.

We are glad to report a happy ending for this couple. They began dating two weeks after Jane's encounter with Jesus. Within a month, John was back home and, together, they fully committed themselves to the rebuilding of their relationship. Today, their marriage is stronger than ever. This is an amazing picture of the power of both unforgiveness and true forgiveness at work!

Some of you are praying:

"God, please heal me."

"Change my husband."

"Change my wife."

"Save our marriage."

If you have not taken the first step and forgiven your spouse for cheating on you, depleting your savings account, lying, or hiding behind a secret addiction, God cannot act on your behalf. It's not that He's not powerful enough or willing. He is! But He won't do anything if you *deny* him by refusing to forgive.

We're not saying that it will come easily, but forgiveness is the key to moving forward in your life and in your marriage. You may or may not feel immediate relief when you say, "I forgive you." Be encouraged, peace will come through the reconciliation process.

Look deep inside your heart. Examine yourself. Do you need to forgive your husband or your wife? Is there anything that might be holding you back from granting forgiveness? Is it more important to hold on to the offense than to operate in faith and begin the healing process? Are you finally ready to let it go?

Once you get before God and release your spouse, you can begin the challenging next step of healing and rebuilding. Know this: The sooner that you can forgive, the sooner that you can experience reconciliation.

ASKING FOR FORGIVENESS

We've spent a lot of time focusing on what to do when your husband or wife has betrayed you. But what if you are the one who cheated or hurt your spouse in some way? How do you go about asking for forgiveness? And how do you forgive yourself?

Never take a halfhearted or self-motivated approach. Don't apologize with an attitude or do it begrudgingly. This isn't genuine. And it won't work.

Don't tell your spouse, "My therapist told me to do this." Or, "In order for me to be well, I need to ask for your forgiveness." Or, "God told me to tell you that I'm sorry."

If you begin the conversation like that, chances are you are not truly sorry. You're just sorry you got caught. I (Darryl) used to think the words *forgive me* or *I'm sorry* would make everything okay and absolve me of wrong. I used to say it to make myself feel better. But there's more to forgiveness than just words. It requires a deep repentance, a turning away from what you did that caused the pain, heartache, and rift.

There is a difference between being genuinely sorry for the harm that you caused your husband or wife and being sorry for yourself. When you're sorry for your actions, you stop doing them. You do what it takes to avoid repeating the hurt.

Godly sorrow is about being genuinely remorseful for your actions. You see your sin through the eyes of God. You become aware of, and sorry for, the damage that you have caused. And you get the help you need, so that you don't do it again.

It's important to note that you can approach your spouse with the proper and genuine posture and still experience rejection. In this case, a few things can happen.

- Your spouse may be too hurt to hear or accept your apology right away.

- Your spouse may say he or she forgives you but may not be able to move any further just yet.

- Your spouse may refuse to forgive you.

If any of the above happens, seek God. Release yourself into God's grace and continue to pray for your spouse and the healing of your relationship. Be mindful of your husband or wife during this time. Don't be resentful and pat yourself on the back for doing your part.

How you behave after asking for forgiveness will evidence the sincerity of your apology and the condition of your heart. Obviously, if you behave in a bitter or nasty way or have an attitude of being inconvenienced by your spouse's need for more time, you are not exhibiting Godly sorrow. You have a hard heart.

Only God can deal with a hard heart. "And I will give you a new heart, and I will put a new spirit in you. I will take out your stony, stubborn heart and give you a tender, responsive heart" (Ezekiel 36:26 NLT). Get in your prayer closet and get your heart right with God.

■

The greatest challenge I (Darryl) ever had was forgiving my father.

Nine months before Tracy and I started writing this book, God told me to do something I never thought I could. I was a guest speaker at a conference one weekend. The night before my talk, I tossed and turned, unable to sleep. My heart was heavy.

I felt the Spirit of the Lord so strongly speak to my heart: "Darryl, you preach this weekend. Then on Sunday, take your brother Ronnie and see your dad. I want you to repent. Tell your father how sorry you are for not allowing him in your life, and ask him for forgiveness."

What? Anxiety set in. I couldn't escape the gnawing in the pit of my stomach. *Ask him to forgive me? Isn't it supposed to be the other way around?* I paced around the room trying to shake off the words. It was impossible. God continued to hound me with His request: *Ask your dad to forgive you.*

I wrestled with God's words until He so gently whispered, "How can I forgive you, if you don't forgive him?"

Point taken.

■

God will always ask you to play your part, not someone else's, in a relationship. You don't need to worry about what others should do, how they should act, or what they should think. God calls you to be responsible for your actions—what you do, what you say, and why you do it.

In truth, I was so bitter from being abused and abandoned by my father, that I had cut him out of my life for over thirty years. I blamed him for everything. I blamed him for leaving me, for not teaching me how to be a man, for not loving me. I had also bad-mouthed him to friends, to the press, to anyone who would listen. Basically, for years I dragged my dad through the mud.

That Sunday morning, my brother Ronnie and I drove to the hospital. My father had been there for a few weeks. He was pretty sick. I was nervous.

What will my dad say when he sees me?

How will I feel when I see him?

What are we going to talk about?

Where do I start?

Can I even do this?

I almost froze when I saw my father in the hospital bed. He was frail. Timid. Weak. Nothing like the violent man I knew as a little boy. But he was so happy to see Ronnie and me, he couldn't stop smiling. We shared small talk, joking and laughing for a while. Then I felt a familiar nudge of the Holy Spirit in my heart.

Do it now.

I looked at Dad and immediately started pouring out my heart. "I just need to tell you that I'm sorry for not letting you into my life. I'm sorry for all the things that I've said about you. I'm sorry for all the wrongs I've done."

As soon as the words came out, I broke down. I laid my head in my father's lap and cried uncontrollably. Tears flowed down his face, as I continued to tell him how sorry I was. "I was wrong. I treated you so bad. Please forgive me."

Immediately, I felt relief. A weight lifted. Peace exploded within me. I felt such a deep love for my dad, a feeling I had never before experienced for him. But the best part of that encounter happened right before my brother and I left. I had the awesome opportunity to lead my dad to the Lord. It was one of the most touching and powerful scenes in my life. Here we were, witnessing the salvation of a man who beat us, told us we were good for nothing, and then ditched us.

God is so good!

FORGIVE YOURSELF

Even if you turn away from the sin that broke your relationship, you may still struggle with forgiving yourself. How is it possible when you caused your husband or wife so much pain? You may constantly wrestle with the guilt and shame of what you've done and have difficulty moving past your sin.

For years I (Tracy) battled with forgiving myself for the addiction that resulted in my surrendering the custody of my children. In my heartache, I chose to deny Christ, reject my faith, and embrace the feelings of unworthiness, sorrow, pain, and bitterness. These feelings morphed into anger, rage, and resentment. I locked my heart in that room of infested sickness. I took my deep-rooted bitterness out on Darryl without even realizing it. Part of my past was bleeding into my marriage.

I (Darryl) had a difficult time forgiving myself partly because I was so dysfunctional and partly because the guilt was overwhelming. But the more I grew in God, the easier it became to accept His grace. I didn't want to live my life in guilt and shame. I wanted to be free.

The same principle that applies to releasing others applies to you as well. Release yourself into the hands of God and receive the power of the cross. Embrace your faith and release the poison. Receive the cleansing, even if you don't feel like it, even if the guilt seems too strong, even if the memory is too painful. Declare by faith that you are forgiven and release yourself.

IT'S TIME TO TAKE THAT STEP

If you're stuck in your marriage, if you wake up every morning and rest your head at night thinking of how your wife hurt you or how your husband broke your heart, forgiveness is your way out! It is the most powerful gift of peace, healing, and freedom that you will ever receive.

Right now, make up your mind that from this day forward, you will never battle with unforgiveness again. Strengthen yourself. Rise up. Be determined. Take back ownership of your life, your joy, and your peace!

You are an imperfect person married to another imperfect person. Offenses will happen. You can't get around them.

Rather than focusing on the awful stuff your husband or wife has done, embrace these truths and begin to practice forgiveness today.

Don't be discouraged if you are sick and tired of trying to work on, battle with, or even study forgiveness. Believe it or not, that means you are ready to make the powerful choice to forgive. Don't miss out on the life He wants you to have. Don't waste another minute stuck in unforgiveness.

Need a little extra help? Or not sure where to start? Here's a simple prayer to get you on your way.

"Father, in the name of Jesus, I forgive _____ by releasing him/her into your hands. I turn over every bitter and heavy feeling to you. I bless _____ and I place my heart into your hands for my healing. I trust you, Holy Spirit, to deliver the wisdom my wife/husband and I need to make the right decisions and to respond properly as we move forward. Do not allow us to get lost in this situation. I turn myself and these circumstances over to you completely. I trust and believe you for everything needed to overcome. In Jesus's name, amen."

SOMETHING TO THINK ABOUT

Search your heart. Ask God to uncover areas in your life where you need to release forgiveness. It might have to do with your spouse. It might not. Whatever the root of unforgiveness, it acts as a barrier that keeps you stuck in your marriage and in your life.

Whether you are harboring bitterness from something someone did to you as a child, as an adult, or in your marriage, repent and invite the Holy Spirit to fill every part of your being. Trust in the Lord to receive the forgiveness you release to Him, and begin to allow the Holy Spirit to work in you to make you whole.

If you're stuck and can't forgive yourself, remember that Jesus Christ has already forgiven you. He died to free you. Do not reject Him. He has showered you with grace, mercy, and forgiveness. He forgives and remembers your sins no more. He loves you that much.

I—yes, I alone—will blot out your sins for my own sake and will never think of them again.

Isaiah 43:25 (NLT)

But he was pierced for our rebellion, crushed for our sins. He was beaten so we could be whole. He was whipped so we could be healed.

Isaiah 53:5 (NLT)

5

The Spouse-in-Waiting

One of the most challenging aspects of being married is being a spouse-in-waiting. This is what you are when your husband or wife has emotionally or even physically checked out and refuses to get well or get right. You are not loved, honored, cherished, or respected by your life partner. Your spouse has left you alone to live and deal with a broken marriage till death do you part. At time, it feels like a slow death.

But there is hope, and there is an answer.

STUCK IN A HOLDING CELL

I (Tracy) know this place well. It was the greatest challenge of my marriage. When we said "I do," I knew about Darryl's past and present conditions. I had spent several years trying to save, change, and rescue him from his addictions, from his money woes, from his legal trouble, from his personal issues, from women.

As I mentioned in chapter 2, I fell in love with Darryl's potential and ignored the harsh realities. I was blind. When I married Darryl, he was clean and sober. What I didn't know was that a part of him did not want to be completely well, whole on the inside. He wasn't ready to surrender and he didn't want to do the work required to be well. The truth became very clear very quickly.

I believed in him more than he believed in himself. I worked harder at his life than he did. I wanted him to be well more than he desired to participate in life. I was set on conquering the sins within him and making him whole.

And I had the faith that believed. I spoke with confidence the declarations that would surely deliver him. I was determined that both of us would be healthy and live happily ever after. I was a fighter by nature and this was a fight I was not going to lose. I protected Darryl, cared for him, rescued him, and even lied for him, day after day, believing that *this* would finally be the day that he came around.

If you are a spouse-in-waiting, you know what day I am talking about. The day your spouse will surrender every part of his or her being to Jesus Christ to be saved and delivered. The day he or she would become well, start showing up, and turn into a good and faithful spouse.

I longed for that day. The day when the addictions would be gone. The day when all the women and infidelities would finally become a distant memory. The day when the money would still be in the bank account. More important, the day two would become one and I would have a real marriage. My husband would be beside me when I woke in the morning. He would transform into a man of God who would serve the Lord, lead his home, and love his wife.

I believed. I begged. I pleaded. I prayed. I longed.

Until, one day, I got tired.

Darryl's multiple infidelities were the biggest betrayals I had to overcome. Adultery is an act of unfaithfulness that affects the heart, mind, body, and soul. But my efforts to out Darryl were pointless, because he didn't care. He wasn't ready to change, which meant he certainly wasn't ready to stop. I had to figure out what to do in the meantime.

Many relationships are similarly deadlocked because of a serious issue. You may struggle because your partner . . .

- is fooling around with someone else

- refuses to get help for or denies an obvious drinking problem or other addiction

- continues to rack up debt and deplete savings because of gambling or out-of-control spending

- struggles with a pornography problem

- is unrepentant of a sin that is self-destructive or damaging to the relationship

- places his or her work, dreams, ministry, or goals before the family's needs

- is cold, unresponsive, disconnected, or disengaged.

I can't tell you how many men and women email or call me seeking advice as to what to do when their spouses continue to engage in destructive, sinful, or selfish activities and refuse to change. Do they stay? Do they get divorced? Do they stay married but separate?

There are more questions. How can you stay in such a situation and still love your spouse? Is that even possible? How do you not lose yourself in the midst of trying situations? If God hasn't released you from the marriage, what should you do in the meantime?

The biggest question we want to address first is, *Should I get divorced?* We don't have the power to make that decision for you. It wouldn't matter if we did. We still don't have the power to do that. God is the only one who can release you from the situation. No one else can. Seek his guidance.

Today, divorce is treated as such a casual thing—unless you are like Darryl and me, who have come to a place where we have seen its devastating effects, especially on kids.

Divorce simply should not be. Yes, there are marriages involving abuse and violence that certainly justify the tearing apart and tearing away of the family unit. However, in modern society, most splits are caused by immaturity, pride, and selfishness.

Jesus himself remarked that we divorce because of our cold, stony hearts. While he was teaching a crowd about the subject, He said this:

> *"So they [husband and wife] are no longer two, but one flesh. Therefore what God has joined together, let no one separate."*
>
> *"Why then," they asked, "did Moses command that a man give his wife a certificate of divorce and send her away?"*

Jesus replied, "Moses permitted you to divorce your wives because your hearts were hard. But it was not this way from the beginning."

Matthew 19:6–8 (NIV)

Divorce affects entire families. Having to choose where to spend holidays and contend with the complexities of visitation are things that children, not just adults, have to deal with. They are introduced into a world of consequences and unfamiliar relationships because their parents couldn't get it right.

Divorce also affects society as a whole. Think about how we contribute to the downfall of mankind with each and every divorce. The consequences are endless.

Immorality

Immaturity

Irresponsibility

Division

Fighting

Legal battles

Legal fees

Anger

Resentment

Poverty

Financial distress due to child support and alimony

Kids torn from the family unit and turning to sex, addictions, and self-harm

Broken hearts

Broken families

Broken homes

Broken communities

Broken world

Maybe this sounds harsh, but it's the reality!

The beauty of God is that He is the God of unlimited chances. Restoration is found in Him. If you and your children have had to experience the pain of a divorce, God is there to meet you in its midst. Embrace his love and forgiveness and move forward in His power.

■

What we can address is an abusive situation. If you or your children are being physically, emotionally, or sexually abused or harmed in any way, safety is your first priority. Get out of harm's way. If possible, work out your marriage from a distance.

When I was a spouse-in-waiting in the early part of our marriage, God taught me a few things that I'll share throughout this chapter. I learned how to love, not leave, Darryl. I learned how to pick myself up and continue to live a healthy, productive, and meaningful life. I learned how to stay married when our relationship lacked life and the emotional and spiritual presence of my other half.

Here's the thing. You can't have a holy, sanctified marriage if both parties aren't living right. It just doesn't work. The relationship is fractured by sin, by selfishness, by betrayal, by darkness. Until that offender stops the cycle of sin and turns away from the destructive behavior, the marriage will stay at a standstill.

Darryl and I were trapped in that holding cell for what seemed like forever. It's not a place God wants or intends any of us to be, but He is faithful. He lifted me out of my despair so I could experience peace and joy—yes, even while my husband was stuck in his sin. He can do the same for you.

It took me a while to embrace this truth and reach out for God. In my case, as is the case for so many, I had to reach out on my own. Darryl would not do it with me. In fact, while I embarked on a journey to live well, he got worse.

YOUR UNSEEN BATTLE

Ephesians 6:12 says, "For our struggle is not against flesh and blood, but against the rulers, against the authorities, against the powers of this dark world and against the spiritual forces of evil in the heavenly realms" (NIV).

My fight was not against my husband. I was fighting something much more powerful, the principalities of darkness that were working through him.

When I realized this, I refused to acknowledge or fight with Darryl over his sin. Fighting sin by fighting a person is useless. You battle against sin in prayer. Until the one you love surrenders to Jesus Christ willingly, you must battle the unseen and give up your spouse to God.

Being a spouse-in-waiting is hard. And it's exhausting. The sleeplessness nights, the constant restlessness in your soul, the tormenting thoughts, the anxiety, loneliness, fear, bitterness, and rejection—all these things eat at you day and night.

You feel like you are the only one in the relationship who gives a hoot. You feel angry for having to do it all yourself. You feel at your wits' end trying to keep things right when your spouse is doing wrong. You feel frustrated, trying to forgive a betrayal that seems to have no end.

This season is also consuming. You can get so focused on

your spouse's addiction, affairs, mistakes, and problems that you fail to realize how vulnerable you are to spiritual attacks. You also fail to recognize how valuable *you* are. You matter.

If your partner is neck deep in the destructiveness of sin, the devil can pat himself on the back for a job well done and turn his focus on you. Then the scheming begins.

How can he, the enemy, get you so distracted by what your husband or wife is doing that you turn away from God? How angry can he make you? How disillusioned? How poisoned?

In these situations, you are his prime target. First Peter 5:8 warns us to "Be alert and of sober mind. Your enemy the devil prowls around like a roaring lion looking for someone to devour" (NIV).

When you take your eyes off God and fix them on how sinful or unfaithful your spouse is, you make yourself vulnerable to spiritual attack. The devil loves this stuff. He is a master of distraction. This is how he operates best. You have to remember that just as God has great plans for you and your marriage, Satan also has a plan. His plan is to steal, kill, and destroy (*see* John 10:10). His goal is to demolish your self-worth, your relationship with God, your commitment to your marriage, and your marriage itself.

This is why it's so important to surrender to God. There is a battle raging within your mental, emotional, spiritual, and even physical being. There is not one part of you that goes untouched during this time. All the wounds, scars, bruises, and hurts you accrue from this painful cycle will remain, *unless* you decide to surrender the sickness, the insanity, the chaos, and the dysfunction to God, then choose to rise above the enemy's plans.

The only person who can ultimately steal your destiny is you. No one else. *You* give it away. *You* let it go. The choice is yours. You can hold on to the baggage and turmoil that comes with being a spouse-in-waiting, or you can give it up to God and get going in your life.

Choose wisely. Your marriage and your destiny may be at stake.

THE PROBLEM WITH DOING YOUR SPOUSE'S WORK

While you can choose to move forward with God, you can't choose your spouse's path. You can't make him or her do anything.

When I married Darryl, I thought I could change him. I thought saying "I do" would be the answer. Many people believe this painful lie.

You cannot change anyone. People have to make their own choice to change. What you can do is pray for your spouse and set a good example. Like the old saying goes, "You can lead a horse to water, but you can't make him drink."

You are not called to save or transform your spouse into a better human being. It's not your job. Sure, you can try. As I did, you can take ownership of all your spouse's actions and consequences, but all you are really doing is creating a codependent relationship. I like the Biblical definition Drs. Cloud and Townsend offer in their book *Boundaries*: "Codependents are boundaryless people who attempt to interrupt God's Law of Sowing and Reaping, by rescuing people from the natural consequences of their actions. This rescuing and the later necessary confronting bring insult and pain to the Codependent."

■

In *Codependent No More*, author Melody Beattie writes, "a Codependent is a person who has let someone else's behavior affect him/her, and is obsessed with controlling the other person's behavior."

Before I surrendered this waiting process to God, I was neck deep in efforts to change Darryl. I chased Darryl in and out of drug houses. I paid his bills. I lied to protect him. I took over his responsibilities. I took ownership of his problems and consequences. I was cleaning up, covering up, and correcting his messes. I call these the three Cs. They are the perfect formula for codependency.

Codependency is a silent killer of relationships. It tells you that all of your efforts are good and are devised to help save and turn a person from destructive ways. Codependency is a sin that results in defeat, because it overvalues the human effort and removes Jesus from the picture.

A codependent relationship is a toxic relationship based on conditional love. Yes, that's right, conditional love. In essence the spouse you are trying to save says, *I will love you only if you meet my demands, settle my chaos, and love me no matter how I treat you.* Definitely not a picture of God-designed love.

People fall in love with codependents because they like to feel needed and important. You become a savior whose job is to straighten out the other person. And the other party only loves you because they need you.

Think about that. There is a big difference between loving someone because they need you and needing someone because they love you. In a codependent relationship, when the need is met, love no longer has a reason to exist, at least not until the next need arises. See the sickness?

When someone needs you because they love you, the relationship is simply based on love. They fall in love with you, not your ability to fix or save them.

A codependent relationship steals your self-worth, passion for life, your daily motivation, your destiny, and your ability to laugh and to love. It robs you of peace and the richness of life. You lose yourself and become sicker than the person that you are trying to save.

Both parties need help. I needed to be delivered from codependency. I put so much focus on Darryl that I could no longer see myself or the God who was trying to save us both.

If, through the road of codependency, you focus on leading, inspiring, teaching, and encouraging your spouse to do the right thing, you will fail. Sick spouses must embrace the journey to wellness themselves. If they do not take ownership of their own lives and responsibilities, you can forget it.

It took me a long time to realize that my goal to make Darryl well was all about me and my desire for happily ever after. It had everything to do with turning him into the man I wanted him to be. When he would change, after my persistent prodding of course, he would make me happy. He would be a perfect husband. This is nothing but a lie from the enemy, which keeps us from taking a look at ourselves and our motives.

Wanting your spouse to stop lying, cheating, and being unfaithful is normal. It's a healthy desire. What is unhealthy is how far you are willing to go to make your spouse well.

What are you willing to put up with? Do you know when to say *no*? Do you have any boundaries or self-restraint? Do you know when to surrender your own efforts to God? Are you enabling your spouse's sins? Are you trying to make the way instead of seeking the Way Maker? Are you trying to work the miracle instead of calling upon the Miracle Worker? Are you losing yourself, your destiny, and your loved ones over your pursuit of your spouse?

When Darryl's personal consequences came at me faster than I could conquer them, I got tired and angry. It got to the point when I was so weary I started entertaining thoughts of my old life, of giving up my faith, and giving up on my marriage. Weariness creates the desire to wander.

It's interesting how much effort I put into trying to change my husband. I did it all.

I! I! I! Me! Me! Me!

Notice it was all about me! Look at me! Look at what I've done to help my husband! Look at my faithfulness, my loyalty, and my love!

My pursuit of Darryl aimed to rescue, save, and change him. I was determined to make it work and get the return on my huge investment.

Here's an eye opener. This is not what God wants you or me to do. We are not defined by the particulars of what somebody else, including your husband or wife, is doing. When you focus on trying to change your spouse, you stop engaging in your own life. You stop living for God. You stop chasing the desires and visions God has imprinted on your heart.

God, not you, has to deal with your spouse. You are responsible only for your change, your freedom, and your life. Your husband or wife is not your homework assignment. Your spouse is God's project, His creation.

SO, WHAT'S YOUR RESPONSIBILITY?

You can choose to lead a life that is healthy and whole or miserable and despairing. Ultimately, I learned to do positive things. I prepared. I made right choices. I focused on my faith. I focused on my relationship with God. I focused on becoming whole.

What should you do when your spouse doesn't stop the cycle of sin?

Build while you believe

When I first found out about Darryl's affairs, I went ballistic. And, for a time, I kept acting crazy. I yelled. Cussed. Threw fits. I did this over everything, not just the infidelities. I constantly exploded over Darryl's spending habits, his disconnection from me, his lack of spiritual leadership, everything.

There I was, a saved woman who loved God, talking trash to her husband. It was pitiful. I was going to church on Sundays, and during the week I was telling Darryl what a sorry-son-of-a-you-know-what-poor-excuse-for-a-man he was. Now, I'm not excusing his behavior. I'm not glossing over the sins he committed and the pains he caused. I'm just saying my furious reactions didn't do a thing to help the situation. As a matter of fact, they made it worse. (Darryl will share his perspective at the end of this chapter.)

Eventually, I became painfully aware of my own condition. My codependent obsession had caused me to disengage from my purpose, my faith, my life. This awareness hit me in a powerful way. I was physically, emotionally, spiritually, mentally, and financially drained. I was losing myself. I was struggling just to get through the day. The nights weren't any better. I knew something had to change. I made the decision to pick myself up and search for my answers with God. They certainly weren't being revealed through the answers I desired in prayer or participation from my husband. I had to face the fact that I was going to have to change even if Darryl did not. I had to surrender to the details that God would give me as the answers to my prayer. I had to let go of how I wanted my prayers to be answered and allow God to deliver His divine details to me.

I didn't know what to do but I knew God would. I did not want another divorce. I was not released by God to leave Darryl. So I hit my knees and asked Him for the answers. While I cried out to God in my prayer closet this phrase came to me clearly: "Tracy, build while you are believing."

I started out by listing all of my fears. As I looked over that list, I knew I had to begin conquering these things, one fear at a time. I was afraid of being alone and financially challenged again. I was fearful of engaging with family, friends, and in life again. I wouldn't be able to lie or cover for Darryl any longer. I would have to simply say that Darryl would not be attending and was dealing with some things at this particular time. I would have to embrace life and learn how to have fun without him by my side. I would allow God to heal and strengthen me. I would have to trust God for everything.

And that's when it finally happened.

I completely surrendered. I turned Darryl and myself over to God. I didn't focus on planning a divorce or on the destruction that was piling up. I simply gave him up and resigned myself to trusting God for everything.

I finally realized I was targeting Darryl and his behaviors instead of seeking God over what was happening. I couldn't love Darryl out of his affairs, addictions, lies, or betrayals. Neither could I scream them out of him or demand he stop. I had to learn how to surrender him and our marriage to God.

Instead of wallowing in fear and insecurity or coming at Darryl with guns blazing, I focused on my faith walk. I made the choice to rise up and participate in my life again.

I started serving in the church. I regularly attended a local Bible study. I volunteered. I went to church social functions. I deliberately placed myself in an atmosphere of faith, around faith-filled women. This is important to note. You must be careful of your environment and associations. Your heart and soul are especially vulnerable to temptations and the influence of others when your marriage is in crisis.

I was determined to stay a woman of faith, dedicated to God and my covenant of marriage. I purposely sought out God in others and made the choice to be around them and to attend events and participate in Godly fun.

I embraced new friendships, healthy ones, grounded in faith. At times I felt uncomfortable in new environments and around people I didn't know. I even wanted to quit and return to my safety zone of isolation, because stepping out was such a dramatic lifestyle change for me. I was not used to being around strong women of faith. I loved Jesus but I was still pretty rough around the edges. I didn't let that stop me. I kept pressing in and moving forward.

My spiritual life also did a one-eighty. I battled my negative feelings and listened to my faith. I opened my heart and every area of my life to God. I invited the Holy Spirit in and asked Him to invade every area of my life.

I remained faithful to God and even faithful to my husband. I didn't cheat on him out of retaliation. I didn't compromise my standards. I still respected him as my husband. I lived by the instruction the apostle Paul offered in 1 Peter 3:1, "Wives, be submissive to your own husbands so that even if any of them are disobedient to the word, they may be won without a word by the behavior of their wives" (NASB). Trust me on this one—actions speak much louder than words.

I never accepted an invitation—not one—to reconnect with an old flame or someone new online or in person, to go out to the club or bar, or to do things that could present me with the slightest hint of temptation. I didn't start spending money like crazy, or adopt an attitude of entitlement that said I deserved to step out of my marriage and into sin. I stayed close to God. Very close.

I made the right choices even when I didn't want to, and right things began to happen. My thinking was being cleansed, healed, and transformed by the Word of God. My heart was being healed as I continued to place it in His hands and not give it away. I began to train and discipline my mind to receive and embrace a positive future.

I began to discover the real me for the very first time. I was able to learn and embrace the truth of the Word of God and began to see myself through the eyes of Jesus. For the first time I was in a healthy, thriving, trusting, loving, forgiving, encouraging, peaceful, and safe relationship. I was with Jesus.

Stop your codependent behavior

Once I recognized my codependence, I took action. I made some serious changes.

I stopped all of the three Cs that brought so much anger and anxiety into my life. The cleanup, the cover-up, and the correction.

I stopped lying for Darryl. I stopped changing my plans to cover up his sins. I stopped cleaning up his messes. I stopped trying to correct him and demand that he change. I simply let it all go. I returned my husband's ownership of his own life, actions, and choices, and I took back mine.

This is an important conversation to have with your spouse. It's part of helping him or her take responsibility. I know this isn't easy to do. But it's necessary. It's the first step to achieving great change, not just in your spouse's life, but in your own as well.

You may say something like, "I'm going to love you, but I'm not going to clean up your life. You are going to have to take responsibility for your own choices. If you do not, the consequences will be yours. I will no longer take ownership of your dysfunction or behaviors. I believe in you but I cannot change you or make you well. I will not enable you or allow you to destroy my life with your sickness. You know what you have to do to get well. I also know what I have to do to get well and to stay well. I choose to be well."

Does this make you uncomfortable? Nervous? Scared? Perhaps you think, "But Tracy, if I do what you're asking, things will get worse! And the effects of my spouse's behavior will swallow up the whole family!"

This is a legitimate fear. But so is the fact that you can't change the consequences of the behavior that he or she won't change. The more you try to clean up, cover up, and correct, the more things will stay the same. You will just become more sick and tired.

Some messes are impossible to clean up. Letting Darryl fall without me picking him up meant that a part of me had to go down with him. When you are married, you are joined to your spouse. Each spouse is affected by what the other does. When the consequences of your partner's mistakes come forth, you must pay for it, too.

I wish I could tell you that at the time of my change I knew in my heart what the outcome of our marriage would be. I didn't. I was just as afraid, angry, sad, and anxious as you may be reading these words.

What I did know, however, was that God is the great God Almighty, and I was going to believe and serve Him. I was not going to walk away from my faith, no matter what my circumstances looked like or turned out to be. God is faithful and I was determined to be faithful to Him. He would lead me the right way. God is who He says He is, and He will do what He says He will do!

I didn't do all these things to manipulate the situation or to force a certain result. I did them because they are the right things to do. They line up with the Word of God. I did what was right and allowed God to do the rest.

Prepare, protect, and plan

I had spent enough time fearfully anticipating what was going to happen next; it was time to face reality. I had to ask myself hard questions about the future, specifically our financial future. The responsibilities were falling on me because my husband had checked out.

What if we lost the house? What if we couldn't pay our bills? Our finances were already a mess and, unless I started making certain decisions to protect our assets, we would lose everything.

I remember the day I sat down with our financial planner. He asked, "Tracy, what would you do if something happened to your husband? How would you care for yourself if he died? Due to his medical history, he cannot get life insurance. You are a young woman with children to think about. What would you do?" His questions made my head hurt. And they punched me in the gut.

I sat in silence at his desk. He continued to drive home the point that the loss of a spouse or his ability to work, provide, or run the household can become anyone's reality. He said, "This is part of my job, Tracy. I have to ask the hard questions and prepare people for possibilities. Just in case. You have to start thinking about these things."

Of course, what he warned me about was already happening. Darryl had not passed on, but he wasn't at home with me either. My marriage was dead.

So, I began to plan.

I counsel many spouses-in-waiting. At the beginning of the first session, I ask them this simple question, "What do you need to do right now to take care of yourself and your family?" Then, I have them write down all of their responsibilities, and they begin to work on and conquer them, one by one.

For me, I needed a job. So I got one. It wasn't enough to pay the bills at first, but it was a start. Entry-level opportunities lead to bigger and better opportunities. If this is something you have to do, don't be fearful or prideful. Just take this first step and allow God to do the rest. This is what it means to trust God while doing your part. Give Him something to work with and the increase will come.

Second, I opened my own bank account and transferred assets out of Darryl's name. I didn't do this to hide or spend money carelessly. I did it because it was the responsible thing to do. Our bills had to be paid. We needed to save money. We needed enough for gas and groceries.

The fact was that Darryl had checked out financially. His behavior and actions depleted our finances and created debt. I had to be responsible. I also did it to protect the future I believed we would have.

Even though fights between us erupted, I didn't. I may have been pushed into a messy corner, but I chose to get out by doing the right thing. A spouse caught in the cycle of sin is usually combative with moods, attitudes, and words. He or she will challenge everything you do and will fuss and fight over every decision you make. Be prepared for this, and don't back down.

All Darryl's behaviors were adding to a negative situation, but I made a positive difference. I began to build while I believed.

Forgive

Unless the cycle of sin has stopped, it's not possible for a marriage to heal. What is possible, however, is to begin the process of healing within you. That's how amazing God is! He will not limit your destiny and your purpose just because your spouse is still involved in that affair, that addiction, that problem, or that sin.

Forgiveness is a part of this equation. It's necessary for you to move on. To live. To laugh. To serve God. If you don't know what to do here, see chapter 4, "Free to Forgive."

Release your bitterness. Release your anger. Release your spouse to God in forgiveness. And continue to journey forward into your new life.

Keep in mind you still have to guard your heart. You cannot look to your spouse for fulfillment, for your needs to be met, or for your trust to be repaired. If he or she is not willing to change, you will participate in the healing of only yourself, not the marriage.

Draw clear boundaries

In situations of adultery, I urge men and women to set physical boundaries. I refused to be physically intimate with my husband until he stopped sleeping around. There was no way he was going to come home from God knows where, get frisky with me, and give me God-knows-what disease.

It is not physically responsible to sleep with someone who is sleeping around. Sexually transmitted diseases are real, even deadly. I chose to not expose myself to this painful possibility of transmittal. It wasn't fair to me or to my children.

Your situation may be different. Set boundaries where necessary. It may be important to educate yourself with the proper legal information regarding spousal responsibilities and obligations. If there is financial destruction, draw the line. (See the story of George and Sandy in chapter 6, "The Truth About Trust.") Separate your bank accounts. Take over the responsibility of spending and saving money. Do not allow finances to be spent on addictions, websites, prostitution, gambling, or any other irresponsible habit or behavior. Your spouse may not choose to stop, but you can choose to stop participating.

Set boundaries on emotional manipulation, too. People stuck in a cycle of sin will verbally and emotionally wear you down. They will try to guilt you into helping them or getting their way. Don't give in. Don't be an enabler.

Stand up. Rise above. Stop feeling bad about yourself or afraid of your spouse. Walk away from arguments. Don't fight back with words when your husband or wife tries to pick fights. Leave the house if you need to. Take a drive. Let the dust settle.

Don't receive negative attention, accusations, or manipulation. What you feed will fester. What you starve will die. I chose to starve Darryl's resistance toward me, and fed my spiritual life. I chose to starve the senseless fights and arguing by stating the true facts and simply walking away. I would no longer give into his manipulative demands or threats of leaving, seeking out another woman, or taking all the finances. I simply told him to do as he saw fit unto God and I in turn trusted God to take care of me and lead me in the right direction. Whatever would be, would be, but my being and my future would be left unto God.

You can forgive your husband or wife a thousand times, but until he or she gets out of that chat room, out of that bedroom, out of that bar, out of wherever, you must draw a line in the sand. Love your spouse, but set up clear boundaries to protect the light in your life and in your home. The darkness does not like the light. Bring the light and the darkness will flee! "Don't let evil conquer you, but conquer evil by doing good" (Romans 12:21 NLT). See the difference?

THE TIDE TURNS

While I continued to build while believing, I prayed for Darryl and chose to see him as the man of God he was created to be. Over time, all the prayers and the daily life decisions I was making were fighting against the darkness and bringing forth the light. Light started to win.

Even though Darryl's behavior did not change overnight, I continued to believe God. I knew He was doing work in my life, in Darryl's, and in our marriage, even during our bleakest times. I gave God the room and liberty to answer my prayers according to His will. I allowed Him to direct my steps.

Unexpectedly, when I started gaining strength in the Lord and living out the hard choices, Darryl started paying attention. He didn't tell me until later what was going on in his mind. What I did notice, however, was that, little by little, he started changing.

He started to pursue Christ and his place and position as a man of God. He began to take responsibility. He stopped rationalizing his choices and making excuses for his behavior. I could tell his pride and ego were fading because he became more quiet and humble. He was not combative and did not pick fights with me. He wouldn't say much, but he started to show up physically.

Without my asking, Darryl started getting up and going to

church with me. He even grabbed my hand as we walked into the sanctuary and held it tight when the preacher would pray. He would bless the food at mealtime and lead our prayer time together. All without prompting.

He handed me his paychecks and asked to look at the budget. He began to study our finances and participate in a plan to get our money back on track. He showed gentleness, kindness, and self-control. Instead of watching television, he would go upstairs, pray, and study the Bible. Many times he would come back down with tears in his eyes. He began to offer me apologies steeped in genuine godly sorrow.

Darryl drew near to me as he drew closer to God. He started to open up about his fears, his anger, his struggles. He committed himself to God, then to me. I wouldn't want it any other way. He needed to be filled with the love of God before he could ever love me.

I didn't question the change or interfere with the process. Darryl didn't make any big promises to me, nor did we analyze the progress together. We simply grabbed each other's hands and started to walk away from where we were, wounded but willing.

We slowly started becoming one, unified as God designed. We started conversing and not fighting. We spoke to one another, not at each other. It was a miracle. An absolute miracle.

BEHAVIOR THAT MAKES A DIFFERENCE

I hated how Tracy used to yell and accuse me of doing things (even if she was right). All it did was push me further and further away from her and deeper and deeper into the wrong things. I stopped listening. It got to be too much. And, besides, it wasn't doing any good.

When she stopped harassing me with the phone calls and such, I started paying attention. I stopped dead in my tracks. My mind was going crazy. Why wasn't she calling me? Why wasn't she texting me? Why wasn't she asking me a barrage of questions when I came home from a trip?

I couldn't help but notice Tracy was changing. I saw her develop a new character, new habits, and a different way of being. Sure, she got mad at me from time to time, but she wouldn't waiver in her faith. Nor would she violate her good character.

I realized she was moving forward. She was growing up. She was changing. She stopped hovering over me. She stopped being concerned about every little detail in my life. She stopped interrogating me. She was leaving me behind.

I couldn't help but respect my wife. When I was still unfaithful, Tracy didn't go out and get another man. She didn't drink or do drugs. I watched her get up at five-thirty every morning to spend time with God. Every single day. Tracy stopped badmouthing me. She was respectful, even when I was out doing bad things. She was always so happy. Even though life sucked for me, she embraced her joy. She lived her life. She was at peace.

The transformation was so crazy that honestly, I became jealous. There were times I asked God why He wouldn't give me what she had. *Why does she feel so good, when I feel so bad?* God showed me that Tracy was free, but I was not. It was then that I finally got to the point where I wanted what she had. I wanted her commitment. I wanted a change. I wanted God.

My wife was waiting while I was still foolish, living on the ego of my past. Boy, what a wake-up call! Her change opened my eyes. I realized that I needed to start becoming a better man and a better husband. I had to start making better choices. I had to stop being so selfish. I had to start changing. Like Tracy, I had to start living in my purpose, not hanging on to my old life.

The most powerful advice I can give to spouses-in-waiting is this: Do not waiver. Live your life. Continue to be faithful to God. Because, you know what? Your spouse is watching. He sees everything you do. He hears everything you say. Even when your marriage seems to be crumbling and you want to give up and satisfy yourself, you are the biggest testimony and example for him. Trust me. He notices what you do.

And, for the husband or wife who is stuck in a cycle of sin? Recognize that you need to change. Come to grips with whatever is hurting you. Deal with the issues that have you so bogged down. Seek help. Seek God. Seek healing. And watch how God is able to turn your life and your marriage around.

■

I (Tracy) have a special place in my heart for the spouse-in-waiting. If this is you, I want to encourage you. All is not lost. There is hope. There is change. There is a better way.

I know how hard it is to resign control. To give up the desire to force your spouse to stay or change, or even to give up being stuck in the process. Sometimes, as awful as your situation is, it's comfortable. It's familiar. It's all you know how to do.

God wants so much more for you. Even though your situation may feel hopeless, God is in the business of restoration.

But it starts with you.

Make the tough choices, the right choices. These will ultimately lead to victory. I cannot tell you what will happen with your marriage. It's not my place. However, I will tell you that when you stay strong and faithful in your relationship with Christ, you will win this battle.

One way or another.

■

Many women have shared their stories with me. Even with a strong, spiritual fight, divorce was their outcome, but not their defeat! God had a plan. I have had the honor of walking through this painful journey with many brave women. Today, they are powerful women with a new lease on life!

Sharon is one of these women. For years Sharon was subjected to the painful behavior and coldness of her addicted husband, Bud. Every day and night of their marriage was uncertain. His behavior was so unpredictable, that they became predictable. The years of womanizing, financial strain, demeaning comments, unemployment, and unloving engagement came to an end.

Sharon called me and asked me for prayer. Through her tears, I lifted her up and ended by asking how I could help her. She told me that she was leaving Bud. He was engaged in yet another affair that he was not going to end. Sharon told me that at that moment she was clear about a new beginning. She felt the peace of God come over. She knew in her heart that she had been released. She shared a comment that caught my attention. She said that she had felt the release from God a long time ago. I asked her, "What was different this time?"

She replied, "I embraced the courage and the strength to actually leave." Sharon had contacted me two years before this life-changing day. I shared my story with her and how I started to build while I was believing. I told her I was building myself back up and getting my life in order. I knew God was doing a new thing within me. He was preparing me for a future with a hope regardless of the outcome of my marriage. Sharon took our conversations to heart and put her prayer life and plan into action. She had started facing her fears and working on herself. She turned Bud over to God completely and surrendered herself to the plan of God. Sharon took a job as a waitress and enrolled in online classes. It was the only job she could get at the time. Sharon had two growing boys to think about, as well. She was determined to build while she was believing.

She was making the hard time count. She changed her focus and redirected her energies into her studies. When she made the decision to leave Bud she was two months away from graduation. She was unable to save very much money, but made enough to keep food on the table and pay the rent. She moved into an apartment with her sons and a friend. Her girlfriend split the rent, and they were able to make ends meet while she finished her education.

I am happy to report that Sharon landed a job with a very well-known soft drink company. Today, she is one of their top marketing representatives and lives in her own home. Her sons have been inspired by their mother's example. One is finishing his sophomore year of high school while the other has entered his junior year of college.

Sharon chose to build while she was believing. She put her total trust in the Lord, leaned not on her own understanding, acknowledged Him in all her ways, and the Lord directed her path. We celebrate God together often, and marvel at His greatness, mercy, and love.

SOMETHING TO THINK ABOUT

Is your spouse still hanging on to that affair? Is she battling an addiction? Has he checked out? Does he or she refuse to surrender to Christ?

What has your journey been like in this meantime? Do you constantly nag? Harp on mistakes? Judge sin? Is every minute of your life consumed with the problems of this unbalanced relationship? Is it difficult for you to take the focus off your spouse?

When your spouse is continuing in a cycle of sin, pray. It's your best chance. Continue to deepen your relationship with God. Get going with your life. Don't get stuck. Don't remain complacent. Don't let the destructive actions of your spouse change your destiny. Don't leave your life behind.

Write down three things you need to do to take responsibility to protect you and your family. (Seeking and completely surrendering to God does not count as one of these things.) Maybe you need to get a job. Maybe you need to say aloud how you intend to end your codependence with your spouse. Maybe you need to clean up your finances. Whatever it is, begin to tackle these items step by step, day by day. Do what you need to do to regain control of your life and your household.

Make the choice today to build while you believe.

part two

WE

6

The Truth About Trust

When I (Darryl) began to allow God to work in my heart, I finally realized how much pain my infidelities were causing Tracy. I saw the damage I had done. I saw the hurt in her eyes. I saw how my actions were causing her to think that she was worthless. I had put her in such a terrible position. My sins finally broke my heart.

It was tough to admit that Tracy had been the only one fighting for our marriage. I meant to be in it only while it lasted. I didn't want that kind of lazy commitment any more. I wanted to fight for our marriage. I wanted to be our family's spiritual leader. I wanted to get into a position with God where He, not my addictions or womanizing, mattered most in my life. I wanted to have a good marriage that lasted.

While my intentions were in the right place, I knew it would take a lot to rebuild the trust between the two of us. I had to prove my change of heart. I couldn't speak empty words and false promises. I had to show Tracy my faithfulness through action. I had to be where I said I would be. I had to do what I said I would do. I had to stop going to certain places and stop hanging out with certain people.

We talked through some things that I could do to help repair our broken trust. I made myself available to her via phone when I wasn't around in person. This was important because I travel a lot and, in the past, I rarely picked up my cell when she called. The more unavailable I was, the more suspicious Tracy became. Unfortunately, her suspicions were spot-on most of the time.

I had to be patient with my wife and give her space and time to heal. It took a while to rebuild our trust, but after a period of consistently doing the right thing, Tracy started to trust me again. And there was no way I was going to mess it up by doing something stupid or foolish. I didn't want my marriage to be at stake any longer.

TIME TO GROW UP

Only when you forgive your spouse can you embark on a journey of rebuilding trust. This is hard because the effects of broken trust—pain, anger, rage, resentment, and heartache—lie in your heart. In a marriage, husband and wife are entrusted to the care of one another. Spouses are called to be men and women of integrity and honor, faithful and trustworthy. If you break or compromise that trust, your relationship suffers. So does your spouse. Broken trust leads to a broken heart.

When trust is broken people say things like:

"I cannot rely on you."

"I cannot trust you to _____."

"I don't believe you'll do the right thing."

We like to define *trust* as *consistency over time*. In other words, doing the right thing over and over. This is why trust takes time to build and especially to rebuild. It doesn't happen overnight, and it doesn't automatically manifest simply because you've forgiven someone.

If your wife has been cheating on you with an old friend, you're going to have difficulty accepting her word. If she tells you she's having lunch with a girlfriend or potential client, you might question whether it's true.

If your husband gambled away your savings account, you're going to have trouble giving him any kind of control over your finances. You'll want to monitor every cent of his income and question every dollar he spends.

There are many kinds of betrayal(s). We're sure your own experiences come to mind without too much thought. The truth is that there is nothing easy about rebuilding trust.

Making a vow to stay together through the good times and the bad doesn't give you a license to treat each other any way you chose. In fact, the covenant promise is to get through the bad times together, not to create bad times through selfish behavior or attitudes. This includes instigating a cycle of resentment because of one spouse's damaging choices.

Sadly, many wounded spouses do exactly that. They sabotage the rebuilding of trust by refusing to join their partner as one and making things right.

If you're still dwelling on past hurts, pains, and heartaches, you have not released these things to God. If you relive and rehash your spouse's offenses day after day, you have not forgiven your spouse, and rebuilding trust will be impossible. Go back and read chapter 4, "Free to Forgive." Without forgiveness, pride and anger will set up shop dead center in the relationship, happy to initiate never-ending quarrels that breed division. We know that place well. Do you?

It's time to grow up and into God's way of doing things. We had to embrace this hard truth. When we made the choice together to rebuild trust, we had to get rid of our pride, entitlement, selfishness, anger, bitterness, and patterns of withholding. We had to come together as one.

We had to grow up if we wanted to save our marriage.

We had to stop bad-mouthing one another.

We had to stop flinging past offenses in each other's face.

We had to stop doing hurtful things just because the other hurt us first.

We had to stop repeating the same argument.

We had to stop giving each other the cold shoulder.

We had to stop giving each other the silent treatment.

We dare you to look at your spouse, embrace your faith, and promise to suit up, show up, and grow up in your marriage. You need this as an individual. Your children also need you to do it. And so does the church.

Sometimes, the truth hurts. This may be one of those times. You may feel convicted for your patterns of deceit, for constantly pushing away your spouse, for instigating fights out of hurt, or for refusing to move on from a past offense.

God is handing you the key to change. Take it. Open yourself up to a new life, a new heart, a new direction. You are worth every bit of God's best in your life and in your marriage.

Dearly beloved, we are gathered here today to encourage you

to change. To go higher! To turn your marriage and mind-set around. By doing your part and relying on the power of God, your marriage will survive and thrive!

TRUST IS A TWO-WAY STREET

When you work on rebuilding your marriage, you have to work with each other to prove your integrity and character. That's right, *with*. Both spouses have to do the work.

You have to get to the root of the betrayal or trust issue. Why did your husband cheat? Why did your wife start drinking? Why did your spouse gamble your assets on a risky investment? Whatever the offense is, you must go deeper than the offense itself. Get down to the *why*.

It's a time for both parties to reflect. We know this can be tough. If your husband had an affair or your wife suffers from an addiction, it's tempting to point out their issues to the exclusion of your own. But you have to include yourself in this journey for it to work.

Reconnecting after a betrayal is not a time for one spouse to judge or crucify the other. It's a time to take your eyes off your spouse and allow God to reveal whether you have contributed to the problem.

Set the actual offense aside for a moment and ask yourself some questions:

Do I shut out my husband?

Do I shut out my wife?

Do I withhold sex?

Do I talk behind my spouse's back?

Am I so deeply preoccupied by the kids, the house, my career, my hobbies, my girls' night, my boys' night, my workout, my job, that I've neglected my relationship?

We are not saying that whatever your spouse did is your fault. Reflecting on your behavior or your way of relating does not excuse your spouse's betrayal. Nor does it mean you should take ownership of your spouse's mistake or failure. We are simply stressing the importance of self-reflection. Embrace this crossroads in your marriage as an opportunity to take a good hard look at your part in the relationship as a whole.

Self-examination in the prayer closet will take you into the core of your heart. When you and your spouse dig deep within yourselves, the process of rebuilding trust can begin. And the remedy will present itself.

FIRST THINGS FIRST

How do you start over with someone you don't even like or can't bear to look at? How is oneness possible when the thought of your spouse's touch brings forth anger instead of deep desire and comfort? How do you learn how to trust in something that has brought you so much pain? How do you express interest in someone who seems to have lost all interest in you? How do you begin again when you don't even know where to begin?

For a little while you will have to do things that seem unnatural and undesirable. You probably won't feel like doing them. But you can't afford to let your feelings rule you any longer. If you do what's right because it's right, not because it feels right, healthy and loving emotions will result.

Trust cannot be rebuilt until the cycle of sin ends. You can forgive your spouse a thousand times, but until that affair ends, or until your wife gets out of that online chat room, or until your husband gets help for that addiction, the process of repair cannot begin.

George and Sandy came to us for help. They couldn't stop fighting over money. From the beginning of their marriage, George entrusted the finances to Sandy. She was responsible for paying the bills, setting aside money for a rainy day, and making deposits into their retirement account. Sandy was happy to take this burden from George. After all, she was good with budgeting and didn't mind the work required to keep it in order. All seemed well.

About five years into their marriage, everything changed. One night, George was sitting at home with their two children when the electricity suddenly went out. As he was making his way downstairs to check the breaker, there was a knock at the front door. It was an employee of the electric company. Without emotion, he informed George their service was being cut off because their account was overdue. The man handed George the bill. It was three months in arrears.

Unbeknownst to George, Sandy had a serious shopping addiction. She refused to wear anything other than name-brand clothes and compulsively shopped online. She would hoard money, hide packages, and eventually got a P.O. Box to receive her purchases, so that her husband wouldn't find out. She started spending more money than they had until dollar by dollar, cent by cent, their bank accounts were depleted.

George found evidence of unpaid bills everywhere. Sandy always had some kind of explanation or excuse for the situation. He grew suspicious. Her apologies were getting old.

When the truth finally came out, the couple was over $120,000 in debt and behind on every bill. They sat in our office for counseling and laid a foreclosure notice on our table.

George spoke quietly and said, "I have no words." He couldn't even begin to digest this secret debt Sandy had accrued over the years. He had trusted her. He had handed every penny over to her, except for a small allowance he allotted himself for expenses and to play golf once a week. He wanted Sandy and the kids to have a comfortable life, and didn't mind her buying nice things. He assumed their finances were taken care of and in order. He was wrong.

Sandy, on the other hand, had much to say. She told us that George didn't understand the loneliness she faced as a housewife. She stayed home and took care of the kids and the house while he was out having fancy lunches and enjoying his high-powered career. Through tears, she expressed her feelings of emptiness and lack of purpose. Shopping was an escape, a way to suppress her feelings.

George had no idea that Sandy felt this way. She had kept those emotions bottled up for years in spite of the cost to their family. But Sandy didn't care. She felt entitled. And she told us that she was not going to stop.

George was devastated. He didn't know what to do. He still loved his wife and wanted to work things out. Sandy wanted her marriage but didn't want to change her behavior. She refused to stop the cycle of sin.

George forgave Sandy, but knew there were some difficult decisions on the horizon. He knew he had to take control of the finances and began to take action. He created separate checking accounts and removed Sandy from the savings account. There was no retirement fund to remove her from, since she had made her way through the entire bundle. Finally, he gave her an allowance based on what she needed for herself and the children.

Sandy didn't take to these steps too kindly. She couldn't stand the new arrangement. She threatened to leave George. She blamed him. She tried to manipulate him. She worked hard to make him feel guilty for the decisions he had made to get the family finances back on track.

One day, George came to our office alone for a scheduled counseling session. Sandy refused to come. He cried as we prayed. George committed to fighting for his marriage. He held fast to his faith and obeyed the wisdom God had given him to correct this mess. He remained faithful to Sandy and his responsibility to do the right thing.

It took a while, but Sandy finally came around. She agreed to face her fears and the loneliness that led to her compulsive and addictive behavior. She set up weekly calls and visits with Tracy to take responsibility for her actions and confront her issues. She worked on herself, created a plan to stabilize her spending habits, and made a commitment to honor her marriage.

She would come in willingly week after week and repeat what she had heard me say about myself so many times. "Tracy, I am here to suit up, show up, and grow up! I am going to get well, and George and I are going to make it!"

We are thrilled to tell you that George and Sandy are together and doing just fine. Though they are still conquering their debt one bill at a time, they did not allow Satan to conquer them.

Forgiveness and personal healing happens between you and God, so you don't need the other party to get onboard for that.

Trust, however, is a two-way street. One party has to agree to work on trusting the other, and the other must agree to take the steps needed to become trustworthy.

We don't know how deep your wounds or betrayals run. In conjunction with practicing our advice, you may consider seeking outside help. Consult with a marriage counselor or see a therapist on your own. Talk to your pastor or gain counsel from experienced mentors.

ON BECOMING TRUSTWORTHY

When you finally admit to hurting your spouse, you may feel all sorts of things—guilt, shame, anger. And there is no doubt that getting your spouse to trust you again will not be an easy task. We're not going to lie. It's tough. It requires work. And a lot of patience. Here's where you can start:

Step 1: Release yourself into the hands of God and receive the working power of the cross

Embrace your faith and release the poison. Receive the cleansing even if you don't feel like it, even if the guilt seems too strong or the memory too painful. Declare by faith that you are forgiven.

Step 2: Recognize that you need a character change

Remember, broken trust is an issue of the heart. You can't become trustworthy by relying on your own integrity or ability.

You need to seek Jesus to cleanse you, the Holy Spirit to restore you, and the word of God to continually transform you. You need to dig deep and determine what led you to the sin. In addition to surrendering to God, read books, meet with a therapist, talk to your pastor. Get to the heart of the matter.

It's important to seek the character change first, not the reconciliation of the relationship. Too often, spouses want to reconnect without resolving the root of the problem. They buy flowers and expensive "I'm sorry" gifts, constantly grovel and beg, and make promises they usually can't keep. If that describes you, you must get to the root of the problem first.

Allow the Holy Spirit to consume you. Invite Him to rule and reign in your heart. Pray that the Holy Spirit will change your character into one that reflects God's image.

Step 3: Set up safeguards

Identify your areas of weakness and your triggers. Make the changes you need to make while seeking God for your character change. (We'll talk more about this in chapter 9)

Don't visit certain websites or watch certain movies. Don't put yourself in situations that make you vulnerable. Don't dine alone with clients or coworkers of the opposite sex. Don't attend certain functions or parties.

Also, don't hide anything. If you want to keep something a secret from your spouse—like who you are going out to lunch with, or a certain text message or e-mail—you know it's something you shouldn't be doing.

I finally got to a place where I kept my cell phone out in the open. I didn't have to hide it from Tracy. My phone used to be full of voice mails and text messages from people whom I should not have been talking to in the first place. But when I had nothing to hide, I didn't care if my wife saw who was calling or texting me. I could leave my cell on a table and walk away for hours.

Don't be afraid to keep your computer on in front of your spouse or your phone nearby. When you are living right, it doesn't matter what your spouse sees. There won't be anything around to call your trust into question. It's important to do what helps your spouse gain a sense of security.

Step 4: Do the right thing; then do it again

Remember, *trust* is consistency over time. In order to rebuild trust, you have to show yourself faithful. While God cleanses you from sin and the Holy Spirit leads you in the day to day, you are responsible for your choices and behaviors.

Seek God regularly and remain faithful to His Word. Attend a life-breathing church. Fill yourself daily with the knowledge and presence of God. And base the decisions you make on God's Word and His leading.

Commit yourself to your marriage. Spend quality time with your spouse. Make him or her feel important. Be a good listener. Affirm your loved one's good qualities and name the things you admire about your husband or wife.

COMING BACK TO TRUST

While Darryl was working on his part, I had some work of my own that I had to do. For one, I had to stop holding him hostage.

There were many times I wanted to throw Darryl's sin in his face, even when he was doing everything right. I was still wounded.

Rehashing the past doesn't do anyone any good. It certainly doesn't play a role in the healing process. There comes a point in time when the blame, the excuses, the fighting, and the revisiting of the offense has to stop.

Instead of damaging our progress by pouring out my anger and accusations upon Darryl, I took them to Christ. It was an exercise in faith. When those bad feelings kicked in, I ran to God and prayed for His grace and peace. I trusted Him to heal my heart because I knew I couldn't do it on my own.

I actually shared those moments with Darryl and even asked him to pray for us during those tough times. Talk about being vulnerable! I tell you what, making that choice was powerful. Darryl chose to honor my request and sought God on our behalf. It took time, but I finally stopped lashing out and igniting yet another painful argument.

I also learned I needed to turn my fears over to God. I was torn by the paralyzing what-if questions.

What if he cheats again?

What if he's not where he says he is?

What if he's lying?

Guess what? I am not Darryl's keeper or his babysitter. I'm his wife. I put my trust in God to heal my heart and to create a genuine change in Darryl's heart.

All this behavior stemmed from a conscious choice on my part to do whatever it took to heal and transform our marriage. I chose to be hopeful for my marriage and leave the suspicions behind. I chose to seek peace. I chose to focus on every ounce of progress instead of focusing on what was left to repair. I chose to

embrace and believe in my husband instead of pushing him away and beating him down with the past. I chose to believe in him by speaking words of life over him and into our marriage, and when I wasn't strong enough to do that I chose to keep my mouth shut. I changed my mind-set and allowed God to change my heart.

WAYS TO START THE PROCESS OF REBUILDING BROKEN TRUST

If you and your spouse are willing to enter into this journey together and the cycle of sin has ended, here are helpful ways to begin the process of rebuilding trust.

Submit to God—both of you

God has to be at the center of your marriage. God needs to heal you, but He can't if you don't let Him in. The one who committed the offense needs healing for the underlying causes of betrayal; the other needs healing from the effects of betrayal. Get into your prayer closets and seek God. Ask him to heal you.

We've mentioned this before, and want to highlight how important it might be for you to seek outside counseling. Find a Christian professional, or even your pastor, who may be able to walk you through your marriage. He or she can help hold you accountable to your spouse and to your marriage. Sometimes, it takes a wise outside source to help initiate and enact the necessary change.

Come together in prayer

When you pray as a married couple, you invite the Holy Spirit to be present. Marriage was never designed to operate without God. And rebuilding trust is not something you can do without Him.

Create new memories

Even after we finally found the right footing, it was hard for me (Tracy) to look at pictures, mementos, and gifts Darryl gave me when our trust was broken. It felt like everything was a lie.

(Never give your spouse I'm-sorry presents. They are permanent reminders of temporary mistakes. You want to give me a beautiful piece of jewelry to apologize for your adultery so whenever I wear it, I can think about what you did? No thanks!)

We wanted to make new memories to replace the old ones. When you and your spouse are rebuilding your marriage, you want to do it against a healthy and positive background. You want to be able to look back at your new beginning with fondness, laughter, and joy.

We started doing new things as a couple to reconnect. It wasn't easy at first. The warm and fuzzy feelings of intimacy didn't immediately appear, but they did eventually catch up.

Our first activity was a visit to the Missouri Botanical Garden. On the way there, we bought disposable cameras. As we soaked up the beauty of the colorful oasis, we took silly pictures of each other. We even asked strangers to take pictures of us together.

On the way back home, we had the photos developed. While we waited, we bought a photo album. We made a pact that night to enter into a lifetime of fresh memories. We were going to fill that photo album with pictures of new events, new places, and new times. We did (and still do).

We took pictures on trips to the zoo and random photos of ourselves at home watching movies. Sometimes, we just took pictures of beautiful scenery to get the focus off ourselves and on God. We took pictures with our children just because.

We also took photos of the opportunities we had to serve others. It was an eye-opening reminder that this world is not about us. We have many snapshots of families affected by autism, homelessness, and children suffering from cancer and other deadly diseases. We realized, and were deeply ashamed of, how selfish we had become, and how we had lost sight of what really matters.

The choice to serve empowered our marriage. We realized how good we were together, as well as the difference we could make in the lives of others. God showed us our effectiveness together as one for Him. We found great fulfillment and joy in something so much greater than ourselves. We were finally operating in the true purpose of our marriage.

That first album we made holds a dear place in our hearts. We look at those pictures to this very day and in amazement say, "Look at what the Good Lord has done!" That one album turned into more than just a collection of albums; it became a lifestyle.

We also did new things together that stretched us. While visiting a local bookstore, we gave each other a challenge. We had to choose a book that we thought the other needed to read. This activity reflected our commitment to grow as individuals and as spouses and to stay teachable. We embraced this challenge with curiosity and a willingness to get to know each other better and to help one another.

This is a powerful exercise. It will give you an immediate reflection of what your spouse needs from you and how they see you. If you agree ahead of time not to be offended, hurt, or defensive about the book your spouse picks, you will grow from the experience.

Now, here's what *not* to do when creating new memories. It's important to avoid doing things and going places with a lot of down time, like a long vacation or dinners out. Don't put yourselves in a position where you just stare at each other and need to force a conversation. Chances are, you probably don't have many positive things to say at this point.

Go bowling. Visit a museum. See a show. Watch a comedian. Find an activity that is fun and will lighten the load, not add to it.

Be mindful of whom you spend time with

Think of yourself as being in marital ICU. You are in a sensitive time and should not engage with people who may not have your (or your spouse's) best interests at heart.

Watch out for friends or family members who stir the pot. They may judge your husband or wife and treat him or her unkindly. They may decide divorce is your best option. They may even suggest that you are entitled to revenge or that you return the favor by acting out yourself.

Not long ago I (Tracy) counseled a woman named Becky who ended her twenty-two-year marriage, following her mother's advice. After discovering her husband's affair, Becky packed up, took their seventeen-year-old son with her, and went to stay with her mother. Mom was appalled, furious, that Becky's husband, Eric, had betrayed her daughter.

Eric begged Becky to come back home. He wanted to save their marriage and work things out. Becky's mother strongly discouraged the reconciliation and encouraged her daughter to get a divorce. Becky followed her mother's promptings.

Their family was torn apart by a bitter divorce that became nasty and drawn out, due to the influence of Becky's mother. Even though Eric gave Becky everything she asked for, her mother encouraged her to go after more. Nothing could ever be enough in her mother's eyes to right this kind of wrong.

Even through the long, legal proceedings, Eric continually pleaded with Becky to come back home. Deep down in her heart she wanted to. She wanted her husband back and her family together again, but she never mustered the strength to resist her mother and stick up for what she really wanted. Becky never stopped listening to her mother's advice.

We strongly believe Eric and Becky could have avoided a divorce. I wonder what would have happened if Becky had not initiated conversations with her mother about Eric. I wonder what would have happened if Becky sought godly advice instead of listening to a bitter woman bent on revenge.

Three years after the divorce was finalized, Eric remarried. Becky still lives with her mother. She visits me to work through the deep pains of regret and sorrow of a life she left behind.

Let this be a lesson to all of us. When things get tough, be very careful who you allow to speak into your life and deliver direction. All advice is not good advice, and it may not even be God's advice. When someone wants to give you his or her two cents, proceed with caution. Trust the Holy Spirit to be your guide and to help you evaluate the counsel of others.

Nurture positive relationships that lift up and edify your

marriage, and avoid the ones that add drama or try to tear it down. Limit the conversations you have with others about your spouse. If someone offers advice you wish to take, make sure it lines up with the Word of God and will benefit your marriage. Suggestions to burn his clothes in the front yard or throw out her shoe collection need not apply.

Other than when you seek professional counsel, keep your marriage problems to yourself. Everyone's got an opinion on how to fix everyone else's problems, but few people have the right answers. I (Darryl) don't care if it's your mom, your dad, your best friend, or your coworker.

If you just had a fight with your spouse, go for a jog. Don't confess every little detail to anyone. Pray about it. Seek God. I learned this lesson from my wife because that's what she did. She didn't talk about our marriage to anyone. If she had a problem, she would pray and turn over our relationship to God.

Decide on three action items you need your spouse to commit to doing

Get honest and suggest three physical things that will help to rebuild trust. Why only three? You do not want to take on more than you can handle. A lengthy list is likely to be overwhelming for both parties. In time, and if necessary, you can build on that list.

If one spouse had an affair with someone at work, he or she may agree to come home right after work and not attend after-hours functions with that person. If a spouse has an issue with money, they may need to agree to submit to a budget for accountability.

While these action items may not entirely eliminate the distrust, it will help cushion the worry and suspicion and get you both on your way.

It's important to note that these suggestions are not demands. You are not forcing your wife or husband to do what you want. These are reasonable and mutually agreed-upon provisions for the purpose of rebuilding trust, not controlling the other against his or her will.

When I (Tracy) thought this through with Darryl, I decided it was important for me to periodically check his phone for inappropriate calls or text messages. I even told him I wanted to carry his cell for an entire random day of my choosing. I needed that. It wasn't going to fix the entire situation, but it was something that would help me.

I also needed boundaries around his Internet use. This included our sharing a joint email account and all passwords, including social media. Finally, Darryl had to be patient in resuming sexual relations with me until I was ready.

This is not a cookie-cutter step. In fact, none of them are. What's important to you and your spouse? What do you need from each other to make it through and begin to rebuild trust? Talk it over. Don't balk at your spouse's suggestions. Seek God. Take your time.

Hold hands and pray

Hold and pray is right! This step helped us so very much. It immediately invites the presence of God into your relationship and shows unity in a spiritual, emotional, and physical way. The posture is one of complete surrender to God. Together, you invite the power of God to invade this situation that you cannot conquer on your own.

When Darryl and I started out he gave me his pinkie finger. I refused the temptation to bicker over this. I chose to embrace it as an opportunity, even if it was only presenting itself as a childish pinkie swear. I took it! I had to be the one to lead the initial prayers. Nothing long or overly fancy. Sixty seconds to ask God for his help and to bless, strengthen, and protect us. I asked God to help us be mindful of one another. To be helpful to one another, not hurtful. After a few days, Darryl took over. He embraced both of my hands and took the lead.

I (Darryl) told my wife that I needed to take my rightful place and take the lead. I prayed for us as a couple, but I went one step further. I prayed over my wife. I dropped my selfishness and embraced the heart through my hands. I gave thanks to God for her and asked God to heal her from my wrongs.

To this day, Tracy and I pray together. There is tremendous power, protection, and breakthrough in this step. This is a step into spiritual intimacy that produces a great reward.

Don't rehash the offense

We don't believe in the statement, "Forgive and forget." Forgive? Absolutely! Though it may be impossible to forget, as you draw closer to God and work with your spouse on rebuilding trust, the memory of the offense will have decreasing power. It may pop up on occasion in your mind and may even stir you, but it will no longer own you. That's why it's important to allow God to heal you. Focus more on Him than on what has been done to you.

In the beginning of our marriage, Tracy often reminded me of my shortcomings and failings. She'd bring up instances where I had lied or denied truths. She'd constantly harp about how I had done this or that. Many times she used my past mistakes and betrayals to make me feel bad. Later, I learned she only did this because she was still hurting. She wasn't well. At the time, her bashing me didn't help a thing. It just made me want to shut down.

Sometimes she even accused me of repeating the offenses. She would constantly hound me. "Where were you?" "With whom?" "Where did you go?" Sometimes her accusations were wrong. And the more she accused me, well, the more I wanted to go out and actually do what she thought I'd done. If she was charging me guilty, I might as well commit the crime.

Don't bring up an offense out of spite or to trigger an emotional reaction from your spouse. This will only reopen the wound and delay the healing process. Alternatively, grab a notebook and spend some time with God—and walk through it with your spouse.

Instead of screaming through the memory with your spouse, go deep with the Holy Spirit. Write down how you feel. Ask God to show you exactly how the offense has hurt you. For example, "You lying, cheating, son-of-a-you-know-what" becomes, "My husband shattered my dreams," or, "This betrayal makes me feel worthless."

Healing takes time. And healing takes work. However, when you replace the negative with the positive, put necessary boundaries in place, and rebuild one step at a time, you and your spouse have the best chance of reconnecting.

WHEN TRUST IS BROKEN,
TURN TO GOD

One of the greatest pieces of advice is found in Proverbs 3:5-6, "Trust in the Lord with all your heart, and lean not on your own understanding; in all your ways acknowledge Him, and He shall direct your paths" (NKJV).

Why should you trust God? Because you can count on Him. He's the only one who will never break your trust. He's the keeper of your heart. He will care for it, treasure it, and keep it in His custody. You can trust God's character. You can trust His integrity. He will never leave you or forsake you. He wants nothing but the best for you.

Read the passages that follow and meditate on the heart and character of God.

"For I know the plans I have for you," says the Lord. "They are plans for good and not for disaster, to give you a future and a hope."

Jeremiah 29:11 (NLT)

Give your burdens to the Lord, and he will take care of you. He will not permit the godly to slip and fall.

Psalm 55:22 (NLT)

Be strong and courageous! Do not be afraid or discouraged. For the Lord your God is with you wherever you go.

Joshua 1:9 (NLT)

When you have been betrayed, your source of comfort and healing needs to be found in God. We believe counseling can do wonders for a broken marriage. But your counselor can't heal you. Nor can your pastor, your best friend, your mentor, or an author of an awesome *New York Times* best-selling book on marriage. Only God can.

> *Humanly speaking, it is impossible. But with God everything is possible.*
>
> Matthew 19:26 (NLT)

Submit to God and allow Him to have His way in your heart. After all, He knows it best. Jeremiah 17:10 tells us that God searches the heart and examines the mind. He knows you inside and out. He knows your past, your present, and your destiny.

You cannot rebuild your marriage on your own, not even if you and your spouse have the best intentions and work real hard on the process. Turn to God, and trust Him to work the necessary things within you, so that you are equipped to reconnect with your spouse.

■

In today's society, people want things *now*. The formula. The five-step plan. The quick fix. The easy method. In truth, rebuilding trust takes time. Work. Effort. Patience. Lots of it.

This team effort requires full participation from both of you. It is a true commitment to one another. There is no room for halfhearted efforts or coldhearted responses. The result will have to withstand the test of time, which requires the power of God.

When we left the past behind and forged ahead to a new level in our marriage, we made a series of right choices. We sought the spiritual solution and carried that into our daily living. We followed through with our commitments to one another. We pursued peace, relied heavily on God, and watched the miracle of trust begin to happen. And it did.

SOMETHING TO THINK ABOUT

If trust is broken in your marriage, what are some steps you can take to rebuild it?

If your spouse has hurt you, what can you do to begin to reconnect? Are you willing to seek counseling as a couple? Are you willing to forgive each other, trust God, and move forward instead of living in the past? Are you willing to create new memories and leave the old behind?

If you have betrayed your spouse, what actions can you take? How can you show yourself trustworthy?

Challenge yourself with these questions. Think long and hard. How can you initiate the process of transforming your marriage in a new way?

7

Mindfulness:
Living an Unselfish Marriage

The Bible tells us that when two people marry, they become one. "Didn't the Lord make you one with your wife? In body and spirit you are his" (Malachi 2:15 NLT).

When we said, "I do," we had a lot—well everything, really—to learn about this principle. With two divorces each, we came into our third marriage the same way we had entered and left our previous marriages—thinking only of number one. Me.

Becoming spouse-minded is challenging for obvious reasons. You and your spouse enter into marriage as individuals. You are two separate beings who think, act, respond, and react differently based on your individual backgrounds, stories, DNA, and gender.

All of a sudden, after wearing a fancy tux or poufy wedding gown and dancing the night away with friends and family, you are expected to focus on one another. The script flips. No more *me*. Hello, *we*!

This can be a shocking change.

The biggest challenge for me (Tracy) was learning to share every part of me: my space, my time, my money, my closet, my decisions, my body, even my moods and attitudes. It was a whole new, difficult world.

Before Darryl came along, I was the man and woman of the house. I took care of the children, made a living, cooked, cleaned, paid the bills, and made every decision, from where the kids went to school to where to live. I played every role: mom, dad, gardener, housekeeper, chef, tutor, counselor, time manager, coach, taxi driver, nurse, boogey-man chaser, and boo-boo kisser. You name it, I did it.

I had major trust issues and had to work hard to live on my own as a single person and as a single mom. It wasn't easy, and I didn't do it all gracefully.

When Darryl arrived on the scene, I had a bit of a problem. I made it very clear that I loved him but I didn't need him to take care of my bills, my house, my children, or me. My defensiveness and controlling attitude came from a place of deep pain. I had been hurt, rejected, and abandoned too many times. I was too scared to depend on anyone other than myself for fear of being disappointed. I figured if Darryl started acting like every other man I had been with—cheating, lying, and controlling—I could kick him out and be just fine on my own. You can see how desperately I needed for God to heal the *me* to be a better *we*.

I (Darryl) married Tracy with the same attitude I bestowed upon my other wives. I was going to do what I wanted, when I wanted, and with whom I wanted. No one was going to tell me what to do. That is, until God got control of my life and I started waking up.

THE STRUGGLE FROM *ME* TO *WE*

The *we* is an endangered species. Many married couples are missing the oneness that makes a marriage strong, healthy, loving, and fun. The desire is present but overshadowed by issues that cause division and distance such as bad moods, attitudes of entitlement, overloaded schedules, and the daily demands and responsibilities of life. And here's the big one: selfishness.

Too many people want the oneness of *we* but want more to hang on to the independence of *me*. These people want to do marriage their own way, on their terms, with their own comforts, dreams, goals, and desires in mind.

But marriage is a sacred covenant between two people unto God, a weighty promise made to Him and to each other. It is an intimate exchange of ourselves. It says, "What's mine is yours and what's yours is mine." Essentially, marriage is the antithesis of selfishness.

Genesis 2:24 tells us that, "A man shall leave his father and his mother, and be joined to his wife; and they shall become one flesh" (NASB). Other translations use the word *cleave* instead of *joined*, which according to *Merriam-Webster* means

1. to adhere closely; stick; cling (usually followed by *to*).

2. to remain faithful (usually followed by *to*); to cleave to one's principles in spite of persecution.

When you marry, you cleave to your spouse. You cleave to her character, good or bad. You cleave to his principles. You cleave to her belief systems. You cleave to his internal makeup. Everything that informs your spouse's character or lack thereof becomes a part of you, adheres to you, and clings to you. This is powerful stuff!

You must leave more than your parents to cleave to your spouse. You must leave behind the past. You must leave behind your preconceived notions, false expectations, damaging mind-sets, and a selfish perspective. You must leave behind your hang-ups, insecurities, and defense mechanisms. You must learn to put away self and start thinking of your spouse.

God designed marriage to be a selfless union. It's not about you—finding *your* soul mate, making *you* feel good, having *your* needs met. It's about having your mate in mind.

What would marriage be like if you woke up every day with your spouse in mind? *What can I do for my wife today? What does my husband need?* If both parties approached the relationship with this mind-set, love would truly take flight and needs would be met.

Now, being spouse minded is not about becoming a doormat or neglecting yourself in the process. What we're talking about is having a heart to serve, and operating in love with kindness, care, and concern.

THE CURE FOR SELFISHNESS— MINDFULNESS

There is a cure for our self-focus: mindfulness.

Being mindful means developing a strong awareness of your spouse's presence in your daily life. You have to be mindful of what you say, how you say it, how you listen, how you engage, what your spouse likes (and doesn't), your moods and tone, and your spouse's moods and tone.

In other words, you have to pay attention.

This is an ongoing, intentional effort that must be practiced for the life of the marriage. Not just once a week. Not just when your wife has a meltdown. Not just when your husband storms out of the house. Not just when your wife is being sweet. Not just when your husband buys you flowers.

You have to be mindful all the time, especially of your differences.

MEN AND WOMEN ARE DIFFERENT

When you begin to work on being more mindful of your spouse and your relationship, you have to understand the particulars of how God designed each gender.

Of course, not all men and women fit into a particular mold. There are certainly exceptions to most rules. Still, there are generalities worth noting.

The wiring of a man

Typically, men feel loved when they are respected, admired, desired, and appreciated. When they are, they become more open to giving and receiving the emotional side of love.

Just because a man is not wired to operate as emotionally as a woman typically does, doesn't mean he lacks an emotional side. He does, and you can tap it through appreciation, peace, and respect.

Watch your husband light up when you say something like, "Honey, I appreciate you and how hard you work. I respect the man that you are and how you take care of our family and me. I am truly honored to be your wife."

Men are physical creatures. They are generally stimulated through sight and physical touch. They also perceive and receive love when their wife physically desires them.

Ladies, your husband needs you physically! Don't always wait for him to initiate sexual intimacy. And, whatever you do, do not act like it's a duty. Making love with your husband as though it's just one more thing to check off your to-do list will shut him down from the inside out. Men desire to be genuinely wanted.

The wiring of a woman

Women are more emotional beings. They tend to engage physically when they feel safe emotionally. A wife feels loved when her spouse really listens to her, is attentive, and is affectionate, gentle, and kind.

When I started to be more mindful of Tracy, I learned a few things. All she wanted from me was my time and attention. She didn't want a diamond necklace or other fancy jewelry. She didn't want roses every week. She didn't want me to go to crazy lengths to do something outrageously romantic for her.

All she wanted was for me to spend time with her.

Once I figured that out, I stepped into action. I took her for long walks. I took her out to dinner. I watched a movie of her choosing with her instead of watching ball games. I still do all these things today.

Men, I want to speak to you from my heart. I know you want your wife to treat you with respect. But let me ask you, are you doing things that demand respect? Are you available to her? Are you providing for your family? Or are you running your own program? Are you shutting her out? Are you hanging out with your buddies at bars or strip clubs instead of coming home? How can you command respect if you are not being respectable?

When men take time out of their lives to focus on their wife, they fill their woman's emotional tank. They help her feel appreciated. They help her feel wanted.

Seriously, what's the big deal, guys? Is it that much to ask you to simply show up? To sit with your wife and spend quality time with her? To take her out of the daily grind and do something fun for a change? To give her some affirmation?

Try it. Just do it. Notice the difference that it makes in how your wife relates to you.

GET TO KNOW YOUR SPOUSE

A great place to begin the practice of being spouse minded is to get to know your spouse more personally and intimately, from the inside out.

What do they like?

What ticks them off?

What refreshes them?

What wipes them out?

What are their love buttons?

What are their hot buttons?

Do you give your spouse what they really want? Or, what you think they want? Or what you want?

When we first married and Darryl was traveling every week, I would spend time cleaning and organizing the house so it would be perfect for his return.

The minute he came off the plane, I'd talk his ear off, giving him a play-by-play of what happened with the kids, in my life, and at home while he was away. I'd detail every piece of furniture I'd dusted, floor I'd mopped, and laundry I'd washed, folded, and put away.

Darryl never seemed to respond with appreciation. In fact, during my chatter, he just zoned out. Meanwhile, I felt offended that my husband was ignoring my hard work and running commentary. The resentment built up each time I continued to give him what I thought he wanted—a long-winded monologue on the home front and a spick-and-span house.

The true definition of insanity was at work. I was doing the same thing over and over and expecting a different result. Finally, I started paying attention.

One day, I simply asked my husband what was wrong and what he truly needed from me. Darryl was quick and eager to respond. It was almost as if he had been waiting for me to ask.

He didn't need to come home to a perfect-looking house with shiny floors, vacuumed rooms, and sparkly bathrooms. He didn't want a play-by-play of what had gone on with the kids or all the problems I encountered and resolved.

You know what he wanted? A home-cooked meal, his dry-cleaning picked up, a quiet house, and some alone time with his wife. That's it! Darryl needs time to unwind. He wants peace. He wants quiet. He wants me. Once he has those things, he can relax and engage in conversation with me about more detailed things. He's happy; I'm happy. It's a win-win.

We recommend reading the book *The 5 Love Languages*. Author Gary Chapman identifies five languages—words of affirmation, quality time, receiving gifts, acts of service, and physical touch—used to express and receive love. When you learn your love language and your spouse's, you will better understand each other and your relationship.

THE ART OF COMPROMISE

When you practice mindfulness, it becomes easier to compromise. This is a huge component in a healthy marriage. Compromise is when two people accept and respect their differences.

It's not about getting your own way. It's not about changing your spouse into who you want them to become. It's not about making him or her see the light of day (or your way).

It's about give and take.

Compromise is a constant force in a healthy relationship. Tension always exists, and sometimes it's pretty strong. One source of contention we had to work through together was our differences in our social habits.

I am not a very social person. I can interact with the multitudes, but really, I'm just a loner. I'd rather be by myself. I love, love, love Tracy's large family and all our friends. But I am not the guy to go to every single event or social gathering or out to dinner every week with other people.

Tracy is the opposite of me. She's a social butterfly. She is very close to her family, and loves spending time with them whenever she can. It was a part of her upbringing and comes naturally to her. I wish I could share this trait, but I don't. It's not in my nature.

My wife and I have had many disagreements about this. In the past, she wanted me to go on every vacation, every trip, and to every family function that popped up on the calendar. But that is not my priority. My concern is providing for my family. Working. Getting up every day and doing what I need to do to take care of us. This was instilled in me as a kid. Our focus as a family was on survival, not going away for the weekend or getting everyone together for a picnic.

I travel a lot, so when I come home, I want to stay home. I don't want to get up and go to this person's birthday party or that family reunion five hours away. It's not that I don't like being around other people, I'm just exhausted by traveling. I want to settle in my haven and have some time to myself to unwind and recharge.

Over time, I realized a part of this need was selfish. I wasn't being attentive to my relationship with Tracy. I was just taking care of me. So, I'm learning to do more things with our families. I'm learning to step out of my comfort zone and be more social. I know how much this means to my wife and how important it is to our marriage.

Now, I'm not saying I go to every single event that Tracy would like. I'm still a work in progress. But I'm trying. And that is what matters.

I (Tracy) take many vacations alone with my family, children, and friends. I never imagined this would be an issue in marriage. In my world, families get together for everything, and spouses just show up, right? It's understood. There is no choice or discussion. At least, that's how I was raised.

In the beginning of our marriage, when Darryl balked at these invitations, I would be hurt. I'd pout. Fuss. Whine. Try to drag him with me. Nothing worked. I begged. I pleaded. Nada. At first I felt resentful. I was tired of his being so selfish. But one day we talked about it. Really talked.

He pointed out how very different our upbringings were. In his household, there wasn't a lot of time or money for activities or fun. Everyone did what they needed to do emotionally, physically, and financially, to make it. He carried this same mentality with him into adulthood and didn't see the need for frequent family get-togethers and other social activities. Finally, I understood.

I now respect and accept Darryl's perspective. I have no issues with attending events without him. I do it with joy. I don't pout, fight, or fuss if he doesn't come along with me. I've learned that though I may not be able to change a situation, I can change how I respond to it.

What's awesome is that Darryl has worked on attending more family affairs. He knows it's important to me. We have come to a place of understanding this difference. We do what works for us and our marriage.

There are times when my husband needs me home with him. I am mindful of this and choose his need over my desire to attend. There is a difference. Darryl and I both value our marriage more highly than our own individual preferences.

What can you do to make things work better in your marriage? In what areas can you give your spouse some slack? How can you relieve some of the tension?

■

When you are mindful of your spouse and marriage, you open the door for a deeper connection. You stop focusing on what you think your spouse is doing wrong and tune in to your partner's heart, and yours.

The rest of this chapter will focus on four components of life in which you can operate with a mindful attitude: your speech, your listening, your environment, and your actions. If you've stopped paying attention, we're going to help you turn the tide.

MINDFUL SPEECH

Guard what you say

I (Tracy) have a strong, bold, and powerful personality. As a preacher and teacher of the Word of God, my gift is carried out through my mouth.

Though I have been blessed with this ability, when I am not mindful of Darryl, or when I am not God-centered, my gift can be my worst enemy. I can hurt with my words. I can become prideful and talk to my husband with disrespect.

Unfortunately, this is a common occurrence in a marriage. I frequently hear couples cut each other down with their words. They make each other the butt of jokes and belittle one another. I'm not pointing fingers; I was guilty.

In the early part of our marriage, our financial situation was a disaster. We were millions of dollars in debt. That's right. Millions! We fought constantly over this. I took a very practical approach to the problem. We needed a budget. We needed to pay our taxes. We needed to pay our bills. Pretty simple goals.

Darryl, however, didn't share my line of thinking. Oh, he understood it was important to be financially responsible, but he had different ideas and less restraint than I. And I'm not proud to say I let him know in very disrespectful ways that I thought he was careless, irresponsible, and foolish. You name it, I probably said it.

This is where I had to learn to watch my mouth. I had to work with Darryl. Instead of yelling at him for making a bad money decision, I had to understand why he had done it. Instead of throwing accusations his way, bad-mouthing him, and nagging at him, I had to step back. And shut up.

I like what the Bible says about this: "A quarrelsome wife is as annoying as constant dripping on a rainy day. Stopping her complaints is like trying to stop the wind or trying to hold something with greased hands" (Proverbs 27:15-16 NLT). Ouch! Oh, boy, was I that quarrelsome wife!

Ultimately, I got to the point at which I stopped yelling and blaming. I listened. I created a safe place for Darryl to talk about money without verbally beating him up. I talked about our budget with a clear head and a calm spirit.

By understanding my husband's frame of mind, we were able to come to a place of agreement. Instead of shooting down his ideas or trying to convince him of my talking points, I invited Darryl to help me lay out a financial plan he could stick to. Guess what? It worked!

If you cut down your partner with your words, even if you're right, you will simply make matters worse. You hurt and disrespect your spouse. You show your level of immaturity.

The same is true about talking badly about your spouse in front of others, ordering him around like a little kid, or demeaning her in front of your children or friends. Nothing good can come from doing these things. You will only push your loved one further away. Use your speech to treat all who live with you, including yourself, with honor and respect. Speak life into the lives of your spouse and children. Affirm them.

And while we're on the subject, stop the negative self-talk. Stop saying things like:

"I'm having such a lousy day."

"I hate my body."

"Boy, I'm such a screw up."

"I can't believe I messed that up again."

When you speak poorly about yourself, you create a discouraging environment without even realizing it.

Guard your tone as well. Sometimes, how you say something can be more destructive than the words themselves. Because of my (Tracy's) strong personality, sometimes what I say comes across mean, judgmental, or overbearing. I may think my tone is normal, but it doesn't sound that way.

It doesn't always just matter what your intentions are, it matters how your husband or wife perceives what you say. If your spouse seems offended by something you say, ask what caused their reaction, then listen without going on the defensive.

Don't fight dirty

Treat the emotional wounds or scars of your spouse with care, patience, and tenderness. Though he or she may have healed from a particularly traumatic, trying, or painful situation, that part of the heart may still be weak or scarred.

If you apply too much pressure to or don't take precautions, you can easily reinjure or reopen that wound. Consider these parts off limits. Don't use them as ammunition to prove a point or win an argument. Don't bring them into a battle just to get the upper hand.

In other words, don't fight dirty.

While in the midst of a busy day at work, I (Tracy) received a phone call from a friend. Amy was talking so fast I could barely understand her. She was spitfire mad and crying uncontrollably.

Once she calmed down, Amy explained that her husband, Joel, had crossed a line in the middle of a heated disagreement. He had called her "a scared little girl that your daddy left behind."

It was a one-liner that took about three seconds to say, but it packed a punch, and it would take a while for Amy to recover. Joel had ripped open an old wound just to make a point. A very painful point.

Have you ever purposely said something hurtful to your spouse?

Something you should have never said?

Something that you regret and can never take back?

Or maybe you've been on the receiving end of a painful comment.

Joel wanted Amy to immediately confront a certain issue regarding her career. Amy was not yet ready and told Joel that she needed more time to pray and prepare. She didn't feel equipped to respond right then and there. And that's when Joel blurted out the comment that cut Amy to the core.

Her first reaction was to lash back at Joel with equally hurtful words, but she didn't. She held her tongue and walked away. Joel was deeply sorry and regretted what he said. He sincerely apologized and Amy forgave him. Joel vowed to be mindful of his speech and the two agreed to press forward.

Still, Amy was deeply hurt. Joel's comment brought back

painful memories that she did not want to entertain. She hadn't thought about her dad or her difficult childhood in a very long time. The argument opened that door.

Bringing up painful or traumatic events when you are mad, hurt, vengeful, teasing, or even supposedly trying to help is never okay. Leave the wounds alone.

Get to the point

Sometimes people talk and talk and talk without saying much, or anything! They skirt over the real issue and end up in the same argument over and over.

Women are notorious for doing this. We are creatures of many words, and men are driven crazy by too many words! They shut down. My (Tracy's) son once told me, "I don't want you to chew my ear off. Just get to the point! I deal with that a lot better. If you go on and on and on, you lose my attention. And I tune out." (Funny, when Darryl heard this, he laughed and gave my son a high five!)

Instead of rambling, complaining, and delivering a lengthy monologue, be specific. If something is bothering you, say:

"When you talk to me like that, it hurts."

"Please do not bring up my past."

"I'd prefer that you call me in advance if you won't be home in time for dinner."

If something requires a more in-depth explanation, think bullet points. Wrap up what you want to say in a few short sentences. For instance:

"I need you to spend more time with the kids. Can you take them to the game on Friday?"

"I would like to have some alone time. Can we do dinner and a movie, just us, next week?"

"Can you be more respectful of my time? I can't work this afternoon, help the kids with their homework, and do the laundry. Can you please help fold the clean clothes?"

Men, sometimes women get frustrated when you offer the minimal response. A little feedback goes a long way. When your wife talks to you about a particular issue or something that is bothering her, and you just nod your head, she probably feels like you're not listening, which means you don't hear or understand her.

Don't tune her out. Listen actively. Engage in her words. You don't have to have a two-hour conversation. Success is as simple as repeating back what she said, verbally acknowledging her points, or asking questions.

It takes two to get to the point. Make it plain. And give feedback.

MINDFUL LISTENING

Listening is an art form. It requires maturity and a mind-set that is fixed on the speaker, not on you. It is about listening to learn, to figure out, to find out, and to receive what is said. It searches for solutions with an open heart and an open mind.

When you enter into conversations this way, you open yourself up to the opportunity for resolution and a deeper intimacy.

It took me (Darryl) a while to understand fully the art of listening. In the beginning of our marriage, I left most of the talking up to Tracy. (She has quite a gift for speech.) When it came to listening, I mostly shut down.

She'd sit by me and gab on and on about our budget, the household, our kids, life, and I'd be off somewhere in another world. Present in body, gone in spirit. Sometimes I think we men have a motor inside of us that knows how to power off when our wives start talking.

Eventually, dialing out stopped working, for me and for our relationship. My desire to shut down was beginning to break down our marriage.

I needed to hear what Tracy was saying. I needed to respond. I needed to interact.

When I opened myself up to her instead of tuning out, our communication reached a new level. Instead of being apathetic, defensive, or arrogant, I became understanding, patient, and confident. I actively listened without assuming I knew where she was coming from.

Our conversations suddenly opened up our understanding. I saw inside Tracy's heart and she saw inside mine. Through the simple act of listening, we learned more about each other. We began to see where the other was coming from. We started recognizing why we acted a certain way or said certain things.

The big thing I learned during this process was what Tracy wanted from me. That, as I mentioned earlier, was simply my time. Me. Because I was traveling so much, she felt disconnected. I finally heard her saying, "I want to hang out with you, Darryl. Let's just do something."

The only way to reach this tipping point in conversation is to be honest with yourself. You have to be vulnerable. I know this is not easy or natural for men to do, but I encourage it. Make time for your wife. Make yourself available. Stop the excuses.

Listen. Don't respond in the middle of a talk. Don't plan what you are going to say when it's your turn. When you do this, nothing gets accomplished. Chances are, you'll both just start yelling over each other. No one will know what anyone is saying.

Men, I encourage you to get out of your head and listen to your wife. Hear her out. If you don't hear her, you won't do anything. And if you don't do anything, your marriage is going to stay stuck.

I know listening doesn't come naturally for most men. And it takes time. Practice. Discipline. If you really want to work on your marriage, learn to listen. One conversation at a time. Train yourself to do this, just as you would train to run a marathon or prepare for a new position at work.

Something happens when you become mindful of listening. Your heart softens. You become drawn to your spouse. You create a place of safety and peace.

Good listening requires patience and practice. Here are some tips to improve your listening skills.

Listen intently

When your husband or wife is talking, listen intently. Don't change your spouse's words, hear what you want to hear, or deliver your own interpretation. Do not turn the tables and make it about you.

Have you ever listened to your husband or wife complain about something you do that annoys, aggravates, or even hurts them? And have you ever shot back by saying something like, "Well, I'm hurt, too! You annoy and aggravate me!"

What just happened? You completely ignored and refused to acknowledge what your spouse said. You made the conversation about you. You robbed yourself of the power and breakthrough that could have evolved had you really listened.

If you don't change the pattern, this behavior will become the norm. It will turn into repetitive arguments that make the heart of your marriage grow cold. You'll never resolve certain issues and will only breed division.

When you listen intently, you create an opportunity to identify a critical need and expose a root issue. You figure out what's wrong. You figure out what your spouse needs. You open yourself and your spouse to finding a solution and developing a closeness that would not have otherwise existed.

Control your emotions

Sometimes it's difficult to identify the need because intense emotions are in the way. You may be so angry, frustrated, or upset you can't even see straight, let alone listen on purpose.

Many couples never get out of this cycle, which also leads to repetitive arguments. Darryl and I have learned to recognize this. When we reach this place of heated emotion, we stop, change course, and head toward solution and resolution.

How do you simply stop? The answer is easy (but hard to do in the beginning when your emotions are all over the place). We cool down, sit down, hold hands, and start praying. We invite the Holy Spirit in to calm us, unite us, and lead us into a solution.

Keep it simple

Sometimes it's hard to listen because the information is confusing. You're not sure what exactly your spouse wants or needs. How many times have you gotten into a lengthy discussion with your husband or wife, then walked away without really having a clue what you talked about?

Sometimes you need to fine-tune your listening by asking a simple question, "What do you need? Can you please be specific?" This prevents another long-winded monologue and never-ending argument. You will help your spouse get right to the point.

MINDFUL ENVIRONMENT

What is the emotional and spiritual temperature of your home?

Do you look forward to coming home?

Does your husband or wife look forward to coming home?

If you've answered *no* or you even hesitate to answer, you've got some work to do. There are two sides to this principle—creating the environment and paying attention to what may be negatively influencing the environment.

We have purposely established a warm, welcoming, and positive home that is also defined by clear boundaries. There are no violent, sexually explicit, or unedifying TV shows, movies, or online activities going on. We keep our home God-centered and view our entertainment and home environment through His eyes.

We are aware that how we speak and act influences our environment. We don't use foul language, call each other names, fight dirty, or ignore each other. We avoid negative self-talk.

Another way to monitor the mood of the home is to begin right when you wake up. How do you greet your husband, your wife, or your kids in the morning? Most people don't pay attention to that stuff, but it's important. A grumpy or bad-tempered attitude sets a certain tone for the entire day, and not a good one.

This is something Darryl and I had to work on. My husband is not a very touchy-feely kind of guy. And he's definitely not a morning person. I, on the other hand, have a naturally energetic and warm personality and love the early part of the day.

I used to wake up and immediately give Darryl a bear hug and say, "Hi, baby! How are you?" He would look at me like I was a three-headed alien. Sometimes, he'd manage to grunt a few syllables in my direction, but he would rarely hug me back; it's just not his natural disposition.

I used to get upset about it, but for the sake of keeping an emotionally level temperature in the home, I started giving him space. I let him wake up and enter into his day at his own pace. I continued being my perky self and allowed him time to get on board. No pressure. Now if I hug him, he'll hug back and sometimes even smile at me.

Give and take.

I know there is a big difference between having a bad morning (or day) and being bad-mannered just because. When you are mindful of your family and the temperature of your home, you will recognize when something is not right. I certainly don't expect my husband or children to appease me with plastic smiles. However, I do expect all of us to help maintain a positive home and to work through whatever disrupts the peace.

Sometimes, you need to give your spouse some space. When Darryl goes through something I can't help him with, the greatest support I can give him is to keep quiet, pray for him, and be mindful from a distance.

If he wants to watch golf instead of talking about what's going on in his head or heart, I don't pout. I understand that he needs time to think and decompress. How I respond to his need will affect our home temperature. This is why maintaining the peace is so important.

Darryl might keep things to himself for a few days or sometimes for weeks. This is one instance in which being mindful of each other is important. If you notice your wife seems depressed for two weeks or your husband has been unusually quiet for the last month, address it.

The point is to be mindful of a major or drastic change in your spouse's behavior, moods or attitudes, not nag at every moment that your spouse seems different.

MINDFUL ACTION

When my wife and I were healing from my betrayals, I realized I needed to get out of my head and start living in love from my heart.

For me, that meant getting into action, actually practicing love. The first thing I needed to do was get rid of my ego. If you can let God tear down your pride, you open yourself up to revelation. You become capable of walking in true love. You have the right understanding. You relate with more compassion.

When you humble yourself before God and grow in faith, everything around you changes. You treat your spouse differently, better. What is really happening is that you become more in tune with him or her.

When I allowed God to strip me of my ego, I became more in sync with Tracy than ever before. I could sit with her and watch television without feeling anxious or wanting to be somewhere else. We laughed more. We held hands more. We joked around more. I become freer in my spirit to love her in action.

You know what loving in action really means for most men? Show up. Be around. Be available. Men need to stop saying, "I can't spend time with my wife because I'm too busy. I'm too stressed. I'm too tired. I don't have the time."

If you want your marriage to be nourished and grow, you have to stop the "I can'ts" and just do what is right.

Get past the hurt.

Release bitterness from a past offense.

Step up and show up.

Take her on special dates.

Be available to her.

Check in with her.

If you're like me and travel a lot, stay in touch with your wife. She shouldn't have to call you all the time. Spare a few minutes, dial her number, and say hello. I know technology today makes it so easy to pound out a few words with our fingers and think of a text or e-mail as deep communication. It isn't. If you can't be around her in person, call.

Most men are driven by and focused on their career. They think that providing for their family is enough. It's not. Your wife desires your time, your attention. And, if you have children, they do too.

Spend time with your family.

Wake up when the kids get up and make breakfast together.

Take your son to his football practice.

Take your daughter to her soccer game.

Get involved in your family's life.

Show up!

Wives, you need to be mindful of your actions as well. Take the focus off yourself and your needs and tune into your husband. Don't nag him, encourage him. Instead of complaining about his flaws, cook his favorite meal. Be more attentive. Offer to turn off your favorite show and instead watch a game with him. Give him a romantic massage.

SIMPLE WAYS TO EXERCISE MINDFULNESS IN EVERY AREA OF MARRIAGE

Observe

Don't be quick to make assumptions, instigate arguments, and throw accusations before having accurate information. Take the time to investigate. Ask yourself questions like these:

What is going on in our household?

Does my wife look tired?

Does my husband seem stressed?

Why did I react so harshly to what my wife said?

When you take the time to dig deep, you learn things you would never have discovered otherwise.

Also, asking questions instead of making assumptions or judgments about your spouse helps you to treat each other with respect.

Be aware of busyness

Attend to your priorities. Everyone can be more loving and less busy. You will always be busy; there is always something going on in life. Working a hundred hours a week will burn you out and pull you apart. Taking time to love, however, will strengthen you and your marriage.

Put God first

We know how important marriage is and how quickly it can fall apart. Being spouse-minded starts with being God-centered. When you're not God-centered, it is so easy to become self-centered. Human nature is always focused on self. That's why it's important to put God first. As Joshua said, "Choose for yourselves this day whom you will serve . . . but as for me and my household, we will serve the Lord" (Joshua 24:15 NIV).

IT'S THE LITTLE THINGS

Catch all the foxes, those little foxes, before they ruin the vineyard of love, for the grapevines are blossoming!

Song of Solomon 2:15 (NLT)

In Biblical times, vineyards were protected by hedges to prevent animals from eating the grapes. When the fruit would start to bud, creatures like little foxes would be on high alert.

These furry animals may look cute and cuddly, but they're members of the wolf family. Don't let their small stature fool you.

Little foxes are wired to attack newly blossomed grapes before they bud into maturity and reach their fullness.

Similarly, little things can attack, eat away at, and over time destroy a marriage. And they need to be dealt with so your vineyard doesn't enter into ruin.

What little things are we talking about? You know, that everyday stuff we do without even realizing: The nagging. The bickering. The irritable moods. The disrespectful chatter. The lack of appreciation. The silent treatment.

Are you so busy you barely have time to connect with your spouse? Do you constantly nag your husband about his honey-do list? Do you favor spending time with your buddies after work rather than going home and having dinner with your family?

Do you often chat with your best friend about how annoying your husband is? Do you tune out your wife when she wants to talk? Do you talk more than you listen? Do you push your husband away whenever he wants to be intimate? Do you immediately isolate yourself when you and your wife have a disagreement? Do you demand your husband do certain things all the time and take him for granted? Have you stopped appreciating your wife's contribution to the household?

Do you often criticize your husband for not buying you flowers? Do you often criticize your wife for not looking like a supermodel? Do you constantly threaten divorce when things get heated? Do you complain a lot? Do you always sulk when you don't get your way? Do you constantly argue your point instead of attempting to compromise? Are you always right? Is your spouse always wrong?

Untended, these little things can lead us directly into big problems. Being continually annoyed with your spouse can lead to an emotional shutdown, which can lead to a desire to escape, which can lead to a romance novel, then a chat room, then an affair.

It's a slow progression, but a progression nonetheless. So, continually practice mindfulness. Catch these little foxes before they cause some serious damage.

SOMETHING TO THINK ABOUT

Are your wheels turning? Are you starting to think of ways you need to exercise less self-focus and become more spouse minded? Where can you begin?

Think of one area in your life where it's time to turn the attention away from yourself and toward your spouse in a loving way. How can you better relate to your partner and recognize what is going on in his or her heart or mind? Ask your spouse to name one thing that you can do to demonstrate your mindfulness in a meaningful way. Put his or her suggestion into practice for a week, then have a conversation about how your behavior has made a difference.

Would listening more or watching how you speak to one another help strengthen each other? Spending more time with each other? Getting to know each other's love language?

Sometimes it helps to look at just one or two things each of you can change to better your marriage.

8

The Divine Blueprint

With four failed marriages between us, the only design we had for our marriage was fighting for our opinions. We would insist that we were right and consequently fight to stand our ground for what we believed, whether it was about raising our children, managing our finances, or spending quality time together. We were both headstrong and bent on carrying out what we thought was right, even if it didn't line up with God's Word.

As a man, I defined my role as head of the household through my own beliefs. I allowed a worldly view to define the man I had become. Consequently, we would get into countless heated arguments that led nowhere.

As we dug spiritually deeper over time, we were both relieved to find solid ground in God's Word.

The Bible poses a profound question in Amos 3:3 that should arrest our attention. "Can two people walk together without agreeing on the direction?" (NLT).

Do you and your spouse frequently get into arguments? Does it seem difficult to be on the same page at times? Do you try to make decisions based on conflicting views or opinions?

When a marriage is weighed down with disagreements, desire for each other begins to dwindle. The passion is threatened and joy slowly disappears. But when, together, you seek God's Word, your marriage will be directed by His instruction.

Not by what the magazines say.

Not by what a talk-show host posits.

Not by your friends' advice.

And not by your own personal opinions.

It is so much easier to let God settle things.

In the Bible, God defines His intentions for the structure of a marriage. His instruction eliminates confusion. Most couples decide what roles to play and what responsibilities to manage based on personal experiences and society's standards. Unfortunately, these opinions may not line up with what God says. That very misalignment will bring about tension in the relationship. Also, opinions may change with circumstances.

Here's the beautiful thing: God doesn't change. He doesn't change His mind. He doesn't change His Word. He doesn't change the truth. We can trust Him and what He says because He is the same yesterday, today, and forever.

Doing marriage God's way is best.

It brings about fulfillment.

It teaches husband and wife how to love each other from a mature, stable, and passionate place.

It creates safety and stability within minds, hearts, and souls.

It provides continual cleansing from sin.

It abolishes fear.

It eliminates confusion.

It replaces the very qualities in you that create tension and conflict in your marriage with patience, perseverance, self-control, and kindness.

When you pursue God, seek His principles, and apply them to your life, He blesses your relationship with your husband or wife. Follow His blueprint and you'll gain solid direction. If you do things His way, you will find your way.

God's basic blueprint for marriage encompasses faith, companionship, household structure, sex, finances, and raising children. He is really good at creating a practical plan.

FAITH

A true and active faith in Jesus Christ is demonstrated by those who pursue holiness by living according to the Bible. As a married couple, God uses that relationship to mold us into the image of Christ, becoming more like Him instead of more like us.

Second Timothy 3:16-17 says this, "All Scripture is inspired by God and is useful to teach us what is true and to make us realize what is wrong in our lives. It corrects us when we are wrong and teaches us to do what is right. God uses it to prepare and equip his people to do every good work" (NLT).

Powerful! The Word of God teaches us truth, corrects us, and equips us. In essence, the Bible is our marriage instruction manual. It equips us to act in the character of Christ and shapes us to be holy.

Faith was not the foundation of my (Tracy's) life or my marriages. I did not have a strong foundation of personal faith. Yes, my wedding ceremonies were led by men of the cloth, and I was raised with an idea of Jesus Christ. But I was not a follower of Jesus Christ. We read from the Bible but the words were not alive to me. I did not allow them to heal, teach, and transform me. I made decisions, raised my kids, and structured my marriage based on how I felt and what I wanted.

I can assure you that, at the time I married, holiness was the furthest thing from my mind. I was scared to death of this word. The definition I created in my own mind—*perfection*—was impossible to live up to. That's because it was based on my own opinions, not truth.

Let us assure you, holiness is not about being perfect; it's about being set apart to follow God, adhere to biblical principles, and reflect His image and likeness to the world. Pursuing holiness is about letting God guide you and give you strength to live His way. God is holy. A holy person lives according to His ways instead of the ways of the world.

Pursuing holiness is going to protect your marriage.

It's going to position your marriage for success.

It's going to bring about purpose in your relationship and not leave the outcome to chance.

God didn't leave you alone to figure out the most important relationship in your life outside of your relationship with Jesus Christ. God will never leave you or abandon you to figure out marriage on your own. He is right beside you, able and willing to lead, guide, and teach you to do what is right.

COMPANIONSHIP

God created marriage for companionship and relief from loneliness. Genesis 2:18 says, "Then the Lord God said, 'It is not good for the man to be alone. I will make a helper who is just right for him.'" (NLT)

Marriage is designed to create partners for life who can help each other through tough times and enjoy life together. God loves relationships! It is the ultimate channel he uses to shape us into His image. And what a better and intimate way to do this than a marriage.

HOUSEHOLD STRUCTURE

We're not going to get into the minutiae of what exactly women need to do in the home and what responsibilities men need to take care of, because God's Word doesn't get into that either. We want to cover the big picture. Trust us, God cares more about what's holding you together than who pays the bills and who takes out the trash.

God's blueprint for husbands

The Bible is pretty clear on the role of a husband. He is first and foremost the spiritual head of the household and is responsible for leading his family to Christ. He is the covering of the family.

For the husband is the head of the wife as Christ is the head of the church, his body, of which he is the Savior. Now as the church submits to Christ, so also wives should submit to their husbands in everything. Husbands, love your wives, just as Christ loved the church and gave himself up for her to make her holy, cleansing her by the washing with water through the word, and to present her to himself as a radiant church, without stain or wrinkle or any other blemish, but holy and blameless. In this same way, husbands ought to love their wives as their own bodies. He who loves his wife loves himself.

Ephesians 5:22–28 (NIV)

A husband must seek God and demonstrate his faith by his actions. Pray with and for your family. Lead your family in prayer. Take them to church. And, most important, live according to God's ways, not your own.

Darryl's actions and faith in God give me protection. He is a strong, godly man and leads our house according to what God says. This takes away my worry. It eases my heart. It soothes my soul.

I love that my husband prays over me. He prays over our children. He leads the blessing over the food. Darryl leads us not just by what he says, but what he does. He guards his heart from temptation by studying the Word and praying. He is no longer a man who is disrespectful with wandering eyes or choosing happy hour over his family. He is a man who works hard and comes home at night. He is mindful of what he watches on television and is quick to change the channel when something inappropriate appears. We see God in Darryl through his choices. What he allows in his life and in our home.

In Western cultures, a man is valued for how big his muscles are, what kind of car he drives, and what tax bracket he's in. Don't be mistaken. The real measure of a man has nothing to do with his job, money, power, or title. A real man is one who obeys God and finds his identity in Christ.

For years, I (Darryl) centered my self-worth on the things of this life, fame, and fortune. But now that I know the truth, I know where my value is found. I know where my identity is found. I know where my faith is found. My house is not what's important. My car is not what's important. My bank account is not what's important. My obedience to God is what is important. That comes first. Then the rest will be established the way it should.

I believe many men have walked away from their responsibility in being a leader in their home. Tracy and I speak all over the country, in churches big and small. I find mostly women in the audiences. Though I'm happy they've come, I'm also disappointed: Where are the men? Where are the strong leaders of the family unit?

It seems that, today, the concept of leadership in the home has changed. It's not about being spiritually driven. It's about being materially driven. It's about making money, having what's bigger and better, getting more. That's not God's design. And I believe that is one of the reasons why families are falling apart and marriages are a mess.

I like to say, "Men, be the head of your family, not a knucklehead."

You husbands must give honor to your wives. Treat your wife with understanding as you live together. She may be weaker than you are, but she is your equal partner in God's gift of new life. Treat her as you should so your prayers will not be hindered.

1 Peter 3:7 (NLT)

Treat your wife with love, care, and concern. Say nice things to her. Speak life over her. Learn how to love her.

I had to learn these things. I am still a work in progress. While I naturally desire to provide for my family and be the spiritual head over my home, I don't know how to love naturally. I am strong in my mind and many times in my heart. So, I make the choice and put forth the effort to love my wife in the little ways.

I honor her in public. I try to be more affectionate than comes naturally to me. I listen to her. Men, lead, but listen as well. Correct, but also encourage. Provide and pour out the love.

Husbands and fathers, your children will learn from your example. You are their greatest example of love. If you are critical, harsh, or absent, you will damage the well-being of every person in your home. Build up your family. That is what will build up your house.

Come on, guys! How difficult is it to compliment your wife just because, send her flowers just because, show her some affection just because (not expecting it to get horizontal), or to just get up and help her when she needs it? Love, honor, and respect her, and do the little things as well as the big things. It will make a world of difference.

After his role as the spiritual leader, a man is the financial provider. The Bible is clear about this responsibility. In fact, it says, "But if anyone does not provide for his relatives, and especially for members of his household, he has denied the faith and is worse than an unbeliever" (1 Timothy 5:8 ESV).

Go out and provide for your family. Take care of them. This is what you are created to do. Does it get tough sometimes? Sure! We all get tired emotionally, physically, and mentally. But get up and do it.

I know some women have no choice but to provide for their family. They have to work and be the breadwinners because their husbands got laid off. We get it. Life happens.

Listen, the Bible doesn't say, "Wives should not work." That's silly. There may even be a mutual agreement between two spouses where the wife is the sole financial provider. That may work, depending on the size of the man's ego and, most important, as long as the husband is without question the spiritual head of the relationship.

If you are unemployed and have been unable to provide for your family through no irresponsibility on your part, don't be discouraged. Keep praying. Keep believing. And keep leading your family in the process. Don't give up. The right opportunity will come.

God's blueprint for wives

Women are created to be their husband's helpmate. God established that from the beginning of time. When He created Adam, He knew something was missing, so He created "a helper" (Genesis 2:18).

Ephesians 5:24 says, "As the church submits to Christ, so you wives should submit to your husbands in everything" (NLT). We know the word *submit* is taboo for many people. It's such a delicate topic because people mistakenly assume God wants women to be barefoot and pregnant while men rule their families with an iron fist. Relax. The Bible doesn't say any of those things.

Submission is not a bad thing. It simply means you are in agreement with and respect your husband. In godly submission, both parties obey and submit to Christ and treat each other as Christ treated and loved the church.

Wives, in the same way submit yourselves to your own husbands so that, if any of them do not believe the word, they may be won over without words by the behavior of their wives.

1 Peter 3:1 (NIV)

God also doesn't tell us it's okay for wives to overpower, overrule, or control their husbands. While it's generally acceptable today for women to wear the pants in the family, women must be careful with their words and actions toward their men.

Be respectful of your husband's position as a leader. Allow him to lead. If you don't, you will strip him of his manhood.

The Bible demands that husbands love their wives. It also demands that wives respect their husbands. "Each one of you also must love his wife as he loves himself, and the wife must respect her husband" (Ephesians 5:33 NIV).

Women, honor and respect your husbands. One way to do this is to speak of him highly. Stop the trash talk! Your husband needs to be able to trust you. He doesn't need you running around telling all your girlfriends his business. Don't make him the butt of your jokes. It's not funny. It's rude, foolish, and causes division in your marriage.

Show your husband honor and respect by speaking to his

greatness. Tell him how much you appreciate him. Thank him for being a spiritual leader and working hard. Honor him by saying these things in public. Compliment your husband in front of others.

Decisions, decisions, decisions

I think the biggest problem women have with the word *submit* is the misperception that they will be shut out of decision making. I hear questions all the time like,

"Does this mean I have no say in my marriage?"

"Does my husband have the final word on everything?"

"Does my opinion even matter at all?"

No, yes, and yes.

Disagreements are a normal and even a healthy part of any marriage. You may have different opinions on where to live, what house to buy, which daycare to enroll your child in, where to spend Christmas this year, what stocks to invest in, and so on. It's ungodly for a husband or wife to demand their way. Couples need to use common sense and godly wisdom to come to an agreement.

If you have a big decision to make, and you and your spouse have completely different trains of thoughts, here are some ways we find resolution with the big picture of submission in mind.

Research your position

Do your homework. Don't just offer a conclusion without proper evidence. Gather the facts. Why do you think your way is best? What is it about your opinion that makes sense? What does God say?

Weigh the pros and cons of each opinion
Ask yourself, "How is this decision going to affect this family positively and negatively?"

Discuss the matter
Don't yell. Don't whine. Don't act like a demanding child and throw a fit. Engage in a calm dialogue about the information you have gathered. See if you can come up with an agreement or solution by which everyone wins.

If after taking these steps you continue to disagree, the husband takes the lead. Again, he does so not because he says so, but because the Bible says he is the spiritual leader. If you have a godly husband who has integrity and is doing the right thing, trust him. It's highly doubtful his intentions are to bamboozle or defy you. More than likely, he has your best interests at heart.

Sometimes a decision can result in a bad outcome. I know a couple that, at the persuasion of the husband, made investments and ended up losing a lot of money. Even though the wife initially wasn't thrilled with the idea and even tried to talk her husband out of it, she didn't say, "I told you so," when it didn't work out. She didn't make him feel bad or question his judgment going forward. In this instance, it was important to forgive and move on.

■

The world paints a very different picture of the sacredness of God's blueprint for marriage. It fights to make men and women equal but with the wrong intention. We are created differently for a reason. Husbands and wives are equally important.

Our individual roles have great power. They're different from each other's so that you can say to your spouse, "I've got your back. What you can't see, I can. What you can't do, I can. Together we can do all things and accomplish anything."

SEX

God clearly states that the purpose of sex in marriage is to produce godly children, protect couples from temptation, and be pleasurable. Yes, you are created to enjoy one another within the confines of marriage. Sex is the most intimate act you can share together. Two become one spiritually, physically, and emotionally, behind closed doors.

God is serious about the marriage bed being active and enjoyable. In fact, the Bible says the only time you should not come together for sex is during brief times of prayer and fasting.

Do not deprive each other of sexual relations, unless you both agree to refrain from sexual intimacy for a limited time so you can give yourselves more completely to prayer. Afterward, you should come together again so that Satan won't be able to tempt you because of your lack of self-control.

1 Corinthians 7:5 (NLT)

The Bible is full of beautiful imagery and language that describes the passion of making love to your spouse and experiencing sexual pleasure and fulfillment from one another. It also says that your body does not belong to you. It belongs to your spouse, as well as to God. You are not to withhold yourself, deprive your spouse, or leave each other sexually unsatisfied.

The wife gives authority over her body to her husband, and the husband gives authority over his body to his wife.

1 Corinthians 7:4 (NLT)

Let him kiss me with the kisses of his mouth—for your love is more delightful than wine. Pleasing is the fragrance of your perfumes; your name is like perfume poured out. No wonder the young women love you! Take me away with you—let us hurry! Let the king bring me into his chambers.

Song of Songs 1:2–4 (NIV)

Yes, we know. This is a cheesy read. But think about the bigger picture. God recognizes your desire for your spouse. The Bible mentions this element of passion precisely because he understands its importance.

God created sex by His design to be pleasurable for both parties. This may come as a shock, but God commands married couples to be passionate, exciting, and sexually fulfilling to one another. It's amazing how gratifying and desirable sex can be when the components of marriage are working properly.

In our counseling practice, we have routinely seen signs of marital trouble first arise in the bedroom. When things outside the bedroom are in turmoil, couples become defensive, withdraw, and begin to lose their desire for each other.

We're talking about problems deeper than not having sex with your spouse because you are tired, have a headache, or have a packed schedule. This is about cutting off your spouse from enjoying the pleasures of intimacy because of offenses.

Here's the deal. When you focus on your relationship with God and treat each other right, you will more freely close the distance between you and your spouse and desire him or her.

Let us make one thing very clear. In no way is it ever okay to make sexual demands, be perverse, or be abusive to your spouse. Making love and sharing the marriage bed is a beautiful *mutual* expression of marital love. Godly couples embrace and experience intimacy in marriage with beauty, enjoyment, love, care, and concern, not with control, domination, or force.

FINANCES

Money problems weigh down many a marriage. In fact, it's the number-one source of stress. We want to raise two points about that.

First, it's the Christian's privilege to tithe. Tithing is a taboo subject, but it's important. In fact, it's a spiritual law. God tells us that a household is protected by the tithe. There should be no argument about the issue. Believers are to put God first in life, marriage, and finance.

I love how *The Message* Bible translation puts Proverbs 3:9-10: "Honor God with everything you own; give him the first and the best." The King James offers, "Honour the Lord with thy substance, and with the firstfruits of all thine increase: So shall thy barns be filled with plenty, and thy presses shall burst out with new wine." Barns and wine signify your financial well-being. If you tithe the first portion of your income, or ten percent, God will protect and increase the rest.

Second, God expects His followers to be good stewards of His money. In Luke 14:28 [NIV] Jesus asks, "Suppose one of you wants to build a tower. Won't you first sit down and estimate the cost to see if you have enough money to complete it?"

Exercise wisdom as it concerns your finances. Don't spend more than you make. Don't buy what you can't afford. Keep your debt to a minimum. Make wise purchases. Create a budget that makes sense and stick to it. Remember Galatians 5:22? In today's self-gratifying society in which everyone is trying to keep up with someone, you definitely need self-control to do these things.

RAISING GODLY CHILDREN

Children are a product of their environment. What we learn at home stays with us for life. Children are very impressionable. They are vulnerable and pure. As parents, you instill the internal, fundamental building blocks of life and love into your children. They are being trained in the covenant of marriage daily through their observance of your own marriage. They will adopt your ways. You are the model of what marriage looks like to your children. What they see you do will formulate their thinking as to what should be done. How we treat one another will be their adopted opinion and perception of love. How we live, love, and interact with one another will deliver their impression of marriage.

A good, godly impression of marriage equips your children to live out a healthy union. It instills confidence in them as children and makes them grow into confident and capable adults. This is the type of relationship we want our children to receive and replicate in their own lives.

Parents' ultimate purpose is to lead their children to Jesus Christ. Some parents have their own agendas in mind for their kids: Be number one in the soccer league. Take first place in the beauty pageants and dance competitions. Get accepted into an Ivy League school. Become a lawyer. Become a politician. Make a ton of money.

We've seen how hard parents drive their children to be the best and stay on top of their game. There is nothing wrong with hard work, ambition, and audacious goals. But there is something wrong with forcing pursuits on your children to make you look good. Or to evidence the greatness of your parenting skills. Or to show them off. And there is something wrong with instilling worldly values on your kids instead of God's truths.

As a parent, your job is to bring God into the picture of their lives first and foremost. Train them in the love of God, show them how to live a life of faith, and teach them to grow up to live for God. In turn, they will become and do what God wants. Maybe it means becoming a lawyer or superstar athlete, but the point is that it will be God's purpose, not theirs and not yours.

If your children have a godly perspective as to who they are, the world is not going to appeal to them as much. If they have a foundation of faith, they are better equipped to deal with obstacles, challenges, and trials. If they understand biblical principles, they will live by a higher standard and for a greater purpose.

Start with the little things. Take them to church. Pray with them. Read the Bible with them. Don't wait until they're older; start young. Instill godly principles in them before they can even talk and walk.

If your children are older or out of your care, do not lose hope. Begin to live for God today. Start where you are and let them begin to see God in you. This is what I (Tracy) had to do and still continue to do.

I wasn't a godly woman when I had my children. Far from it. They weren't raised in a godly home and taught all the things that we discuss here. It wasn't until later, in their teenage years, that they were introduced to faith.

Because of our multiple divorces, our children were not in our custody or care for a long time. Darryl and I started by simply praying for them, even when we couldn't visit them or speak with them. There is power in prayer, my dear friend.

Our children see the dramatic change in both of our lives. They know that God is real. A desire to know God is stirred in them this very day!

Speak life into your children. Tell them about their greatness in God. Tell them that they are awesome, strong, wonderfully and beautifully made. Tell them that God created them with special talents and abilities. Tell them that He has set them apart for a unique purpose only they can fulfill.

I wish that I had done this sooner. Had I been equipped with this knowledge when I was first pregnant, I would have prayed over my children when they were in the womb. Trust me, it's never too early. The foundation you create for your children will shape them as they grow up.

The best way to raise godly kids is to model a godly life. Let your children see God in you by the way you live, operate your household, and run your life. You are their greatest example and form their opinion of who God is and how we should live.

If God is not your first priority, how will they know to put Him first? How can you expect them to live according to biblical principles if you talk badly about people, your neighbor, flip the bird when someone cuts you off on the road, ignore serving those in need, and watch TV shows or movies that are not life building or edifying?

Your kids will not go to church if you criticize the church, if you do not go, take them with you, or go begrudgingly. Find a church that you can call home. One that is Bible-based and spirit-filled. One where you enjoy spending your Sunday mornings. One where you can serve. One where you can connect with others.

Want to instill a prayer life in your kids? Teach them by praying with them. Want them to live a passionate faith life? Build up yours. Present them with the joy of faith through your own quiet time with God.

Your kids will follow your example, even and especially when you think they're not looking. You paint their very first picture of God. You are their very first experience of God. You set the standard and help to form their opinion.

PASSION *IS* PART OF THE PACKAGE

Does it sound as though we are overspiritualizing marriage at the cost of the killing off the butterflies in your stomach? I hope not!

We realize attraction is part of the equation. Here's the thing—when you understand God's purpose for your relationship, when you lay down what *you* want or hope to gain through your spouse, when you focus on God, the other stuff will follow!

You'll start to experience passion and excitement. You'll look at your partner in a new way. You'll even fall in love all over again.

This may sound crazy if you can't stand looking at your husband or wife right now, but be open to the possibility. When your character is right and you are treating each other right, you'll find you want to meet your partner's needs.

You'll want to buy her roses. You'll want to give him a massage. You'll want to plan a romantic getaway weekend. You'll want to surprise him with a three-course meal. The surface expectations that are pleasant and fun and feel good will come after you change your mind-set to a God-designed perspective.

SOMETHING TO THINK ABOUT

Think about the current state of your marriage and compare it with God's blueprint. What are some differences? What is similar? What needs to be changed?

Perhaps, men, you need to start treating your wife with more understanding and affection. Maybe, wives, you need to start honoring your husband. Do you need to come to grips with your financial situation? Give God His due? Create a realistic budget? Do you need to incorporate faith into your home life? Start learning about God and experiencing Him by going to church? Start serving?

Together, write down three ways each of you can align your marriage with God's blueprint.

9

Temptation: The Fall of All

Until God did a work in my life and I began truly living by His principles, women were my greatest temptation.

I'm not proud to admit that in beginning of my marriage to Tracy, I strayed. I had multiple affairs. I fell into temptation so easily, almost without thinking. It wasn't because I didn't think my wife was good enough. She was. I was just so used to a certain lifestyle, in particular having a different kind of woman whenever I wanted. It was like a flavor-of-the-week club.

I had an appetite for indulging my flesh. I'm sure it was different for me than the average man. Because of my celebrity and athletic background, I was always in the limelight, surrounded by women who would come on to me and by people who wouldn't say no to me. Knowing I could have almost any woman I wanted was a huge motivation to do just that.

Yes, it was sick. And twisted. And it almost destroyed my marriage. I am deeply, deeply ashamed of that.

Affairs are no joke. They are serious. And they are dangerous. They destroy your character. They can destroy your marriage. They can destroy your relationship with your spouse, your children, and even God.

I think the biggest reason that I constantly fell into temptation with women was that I was insecure. I was confident in my athletic abilities. I was confident I could provide for my family. I was confident that I could make a living, and a good one at that.

But I had self-esteem issues. I questioned my self-worth. I grew up with a dad who had always hammered into me that I was worthless, and I never found my identity in Christ.

I've learned that most men cheat for three reasons. First, like me, they have low self-esteem. They can look good in their clothes, in their car, in their house, or in their position at work and still battle with a poor self-image. As long as they look to things outside of God to boost their self-confidence, they will always struggle.

Second, men are looking for excitement. They are chasing the thrill. They are caught up in thinking there is someone better out there for them than their wife. Someone prettier, thinner, younger, more passionate, more loving, more whatever. The funny thing is—and trust me, I know what I'm talking about—there is nothing for them in the chase but trouble.

Men drift away from their relationships and get lost because they are convinced life is more exciting, fun, and sexy somewhere other than in their home. Guess what? It's not. When you are not focused on your marriage, unhealthy interests in other things will drag you down, deeper and deeper.

I know many good men who have been brought down in their reputation, their career, and their family because they didn't say no to temptation. And for what? More heartache, more pain, and more problems.

Third, I find that most men have affairs because they can. Sometimes it's that simple and, I realize, very discouraging to women. Here's where selfishness rears its ugly head. When you operate with a just-because-I-can attitude, you're operating in selfishness. You are only concerned with doing whatever you want. That's where my heart was.

When I had affairs, I was constantly hurting people. I hurt my wives. I hurt my children. I hurt those who were closest to me. I caused nothing but pain for the sake of doing what I wanted to do. When life is about me-me-me, you tend to do things you shouldn't and that aren't right because no one is looking. And because you think you won't get caught.

When you operate according to God's principles and not your selfishness, you realize that your character matters whether or not anyone else is watching. It's called *integrity*. You do the right thing at all times, in public and in private, because you live not for yourself, but for God.

Everyone has the ability and the authority to walk away from tempting things that are detrimental to family and self. Unfortunately, if you are not well, whole, or just plain mindful, you will walk right into temptation. You will step into a compromising situation that will open Pandora's Box.

One minute, you're staring at a hot chick. The next, you can't get her out of your mind. Then you start fantasizing. You pull out a computer, check out a porn site, and visit a few chat rooms. Before you know it, you are having an affair.

The difference between my life today and my past is that now the power of God operates in me. Knowing that fuels me to do the right thing. I choose to say no. I choose to walk away. I choose to stay away from things that will cause ruin. My life is about my character. My wife. My family. God. I honor those relationships and don't allow myself to be seduced by the world.

I've been in the thick of temptation for years. I've seen the destruction. I know the devastation. I understand the pain and suffering it produces in a marriage. It's disgusting. Truly disgusting.

I am so grateful to God for changing my life, opening my eyes, and bringing me to a place where women don't faze me. I would never put Tracy through that hell again. My love and respect for her and for God are too strong.

FALSE PROMISES

Temptation means to be enticed and allured by something attractive or desirable, especially by what can cause ultimate destruction. It's a powerful force that leads away from God and into the world of deception, lust, and harm. It glamorizes sin and entices the appetites of ungodly desire.

Temptation will promise you pleasure, passion, power, or relief. In fact, it has to deliver an appealing guarantee of some sort or else it wouldn't be attractive, and you wouldn't fall for it. It has to look, sound, taste, smell, or feel good. It has to appeal to your five senses and your soul. (Soul is your mind, will, and emotions.)

The promises of temptation are lies of the enemy. Here's the thing. The lusts of the flesh can never be satisfied. Your body, mind, and will constantly crave more. It's never enough—not just one woman, one drink, one win, one hit, one purchase. Human desires are untamed and without limits. It reminds me of a T-shirt slogan I've seen. Front: Come to the dark side. We have cookies. Back: Welcome to the dark side. Are you surprised we lied about the cookies?

This highly sensory world constantly bombards people with messages and images that appeal to sinful desires. Even the pressures of simple daily living can make couples tired, stressed, and unfulfilled, catalysts for seeking immediate, though temporary, satisfaction.

You can be tempted to do a slew of things that can lead to a breakdown of a marriage. Cheating is not the only medium.

You can be enticed to have an emotional affair. Many people believe that cheating is defined only as a physical, sexual affair. The Bible states that we have committed adultery even with one impure thought. Sharing, chatting, or engaging in emotional dialogue with the opposite sex is wrong. It is emotional cheating. This type of dialogue leads into the next stage of the physical affair: the sexual encounter.

You can battle an addiction to drugs, alcohol, or food.

You can be hooked on pornography.

You can be a poor steward of your money.

You can be tempted to revisit old habits that once undermined your heart, your soul, and your life.

And what about the temptation to dishonor your spouse with your speech?

To overlook your spouse and focus on self?

To spend part of that budgeted savings on a new pair of shoes you don't need?

To create that secret email account?

To exchange so-called innocent flirtatious comments via Facebook?

Temptations can begin in very subtle ways.

An innocent invitation to lunch. A soft whisper. An enticing scent. A gentle touch. A lingering hug. A kind word. A listening ear. A persistent presence. A harmless chat over drinks. (Hmm, sounds like we're talking about little foxes, doesn't it?) But these little things over time can lead you into irresistible opportunities.

Before you know it, you find yourself saying, "My God! What have I done? How did this happen? How did I get here?"

The person, the act, the indulgence that once promised passion, power, pleasure, or relief turns into pain, heartache, deception, destruction, and defeat. Your character crumbles. Your integrity collapses. Funny how temptation doesn't inform or prepare you for its consequences.

Regardless of where it comes from or what it looks like, temptation is temptation. And if you fall prey to its seductive beckoning, you're headed down a road toward a whole lot of trouble. This is why Jesus told us to pray against temptation. "And lead us not into temptation, but deliver us from the evil one." (Matthew 6:13 NIV)

NO ONE IS IMMUNE

As a Christian, you will be challenged by temptation. If you think you're immune to doing something that can destroy your marriage, your sobriety, or your financial situation, think again.

Many Christians are naive and think that just because they read the Bible, pray, and love God, they are not susceptible to being tempted. This is not true. Everyone is at risk. Given the right circumstances, anyone can be vulnerable. You cannot be so proud, thinking you are strong enough to resist every temptation. You must be on guard at all times.

When you surrender your life to Jesus and invite the Holy Spirit to dwell within you, you embrace godly power. When you are weak, He is strong. He equips you with the power you need to say no.

I (Tracy) have learned that if I continually abide with God, He will change my desires. You may struggle with a particular addiction, temptation, or thought, but the more you plug into Him, the less that desire will scream at you, and the better equipped you will be to walk away from the temptation.

Stay alert! Watch out for your great enemy, the devil.
He prowls around like a roaring lion, looking for someone
  to devour.

1 Peter 5:8 (NLT)

THE FALL OF THE HUMAN RACE

Temptation took root in the beginning of time when Adam and Eve did the one thing God told them not to do. Genesis 3 recounts how Satan, a fallen angel who appears as a wily serpent, convinces Eve to eat the forbidden fruit.

In this passage, Satan engages the senses of the soul. God has offered Adam and Eve several ways of escape, but they take none of these.

Take a look at this setup by the enemy:

Now the serpent was more crafty than any of the wild animals the Lord God had made. He said to the woman, "Did God really say, 'You must not eat from any tree in the garden'?"

The woman said to the serpent, "We may eat fruit from the trees in the garden, but God did say, 'You must not eat fruit from the tree that is in the middle of the garden, and you must not touch it, or you will die.'"

"You will not certainly die," the serpent said to the woman. "For God knows that when you eat from it your eyes will be opened, and you will be like God, knowing good and evil."

When the woman saw that the fruit of the tree was good for food and pleasing to the eye, and also desirable for gaining wisdom, she took some and ate it. She also gave some to her husband, who was with her, and he ate it. Then the eyes of both of them were opened, and they realized they were naked; so they sewed fig leaves together and made coverings for themselves.

Genesis 3:1-7 (NIV)

So, what happened? How could two people who were in constant fellowship with God fall into temptation? How could they be so easily led astray?

After all, Adam and Eve had no character defects or internal issues. They weren't pressured by society. They didn't fall on hard times. They didn't have money problems. They didn't have workplace drama or parenting concerns.

They were connected with God. They walked with Him every day. They were operating in their purpose. They were reflections of their Creator's glory. They knew their identity was in Him. They knew the Word, which was spoken to them daily by God.

What went wrong?

This couple did not flee from the devil and his enticements. They allowed ungodly desire to take root in their hearts and grow. They did not remove themselves from the situation. They acted out. They disobeyed. And they fell.

Eve engaged with the enemy, who initiated the encounter by testing God's word. She allowed herself to doubt her Maker and question His authority. She mused that perhaps the serpent was right. Maybe her ways were better than those of God.

Yeah, that seems about right. I need to do my own thing. I need to follow my heart, my leading, my direction, my warning. I mean, really, I know best, right? Maybe this sounds like something you've been saying.

Make no mistake. Eve had the opportunity to respond with truth and escape the devil's advances. But she didn't. She kept entertaining those thoughts. She let him entice her sense of sight and taste, the beautiful and delicious fruit to which her eyes were drawn. She did not interrupt the temptation. Instead, she took a juicy bite and gave it to Adam to do the same.

BEWARE THE CONSEQUENCES

As a result of their disobedience, Adam and Eve were kicked out of the garden, out of God's presence. They had no choice in the matter. Eden was a holy place, a utopia free of sin and its aftermath. Now that they had a sinful nature, the couple couldn't stay. They had to leave.

Sin cannot exist in the presence of the Holy God. That is why we all need a Savior, Jesus Christ. His blood washes away every sin—past, present, and future. What an amazing truth! For those of us who believe in Him, Jesus sees us just as if we never sinned.

While there is no condemnation for those who abide in Him, there are consequences. Adam and Eve's consequences were far reaching, extending through every generation of the human race.

When we sin, when we fall into temptation, we are not the only ones affected by it. Our children, our families, and our friends all experience the fallout.

When I (Tracy) was an addict, I hurt my children, my family, and my friends through my lies, my apathy, and my inability to love.

When I divorced and entered into ungodly relationships, my loved ones were also impacted. My actions created division in my family. My bad choices uprooted the lives of my children.

Participation in temptation, in sin, in selfishness, in destructive behavior, hurts many beyond the scope of self. Hypocrisy turns people away from Christ, especially those who are not strong in their faith or have no faith at all.

And what about Jesus Christ? When we indulge in our sinful nature and say yes to the things we should say no to, our actions destroy His witness within us. We tarnish His reputation. And we tarnish the faith.

But wait. There's a light ahead. We want you to see it.

Note that God loved Adam and Eve in spite of their sin. He didn't abandon them. Before God sent them off, He actually clothed them. He covered them. He provided for them.

The important thing to remember is that God loves the sinner and hates the sin. He hates sin because it harms us. It brings forth division, destruction, and defeat. It tears us away from Him and those we love.

Listen, we know the pleasures of our flesh feel good—whether it's downing that drink, sharing that bed, binging on sugar, or purchasing that item. But it's a temporary fix for a permanent problem.

God is not in the business of taking away good things from us. On the contrary, He wants to keep us from what will harm our marriage, us, and others.

WHERE DOES TEMPTATION COME FROM?

It's important to note that God did not create temptation. "No one should say, 'God is tempting me.' For God cannot be tempted by evil, nor does he tempt anyone; but each person is tempted when they are dragged away by their own evil desire and enticed" (James 1:13 NIV).

God doesn't dangle a willing attractive man or woman in front of you. He doesn't put that gin and tonic in your hands. He doesn't offer you an invitation to that strip club, that bar, or that party. He doesn't sit you down in front of that TV show or movie. He doesn't put those way-too-expensive shoes on your feet.

Temptation is a setup by the enemy to lead you away from God. It is designed to tear down your character. When you succumb to the pressure, the devil knows you will experience pain and consequences, instead of fulfilling your purpose and receiving your promotion in faith and in life.

God, on the other hand, allows temptation to test and strengthen your character. When you resist the trap, you increase your level of faith, your integrity rises, and you become better equipped and stay on course to fulfill God's plan for your life. You also grow as a spouse by growing in character.

You embrace godly desires that will drive you further into the things of God and protect you from the evils of this world. "Delight yourself in the Lord; and He will give you the desires of your heart" (Psalm 37:4 NASB). Godly desires produce divine results—like a strong, healthy, and lasting marriage.

HOW TO RESIST TEMPTATION

With God's help, you can avoid falling into temptation. You can say no. You can use self-control. You can be self-disciplined.

Paul gave encouraging news in 1 Corinthians 10:13. "The temptations in your life are no different from what others experience. And God is faithful. He will not allow the temptation to be more than you can stand. When you are tempted, he will show you a way out so that you can endure" (NLT).

Let's examine four ways you can avoid falling into temptation.

Guard your gates

Be aware of how temptation affects the five senses—smell, touch, hearing, seeing, and taste. Remember how Eve was seduced by the look and taste of the delicious fruit?

It's amazing how desire can be stirred by the scent of perfume, a glass of wine, or an aromatic bakery. How hearts beat faster after a touch on the arm, a tight embrace, or the texture of a pricey leather handbag. How a certain song, a certain voice, a certain word can trigger a fantasy. How eyes are drawn to that TV commercial, that beautiful woman, that Facebook profile. How a bite of that red velvet cake, a hint of that white powder, or a puff of that cigarette can cause stumbling.

Guard your gates, people. When you allow your senses to run unchecked, you are vulnerable to temptation.

Put the glass down.

Turn off the movie.

Walk out of the store.

When temptation comes knocking, don't open the gates. Guard them. Keep them shut, turn away from the knock, and stay on the right path.

To this day, the smell of wine stirs a hint of temptation in me (Tracy). It is not strong enough to make me want to drink, but it's still powerful. The subtle scent arrests my attention. If I so much as entertain the desire, I know where it'll lead. I'm not naive. I do not make excuses and I do not compromise. I safeguard myself.

I have left dinners and walked out of parties where the temptation to drink is before me. If I'm at a restaurant, I turn over my wine glass as soon as I sit down. I address this immediately. I don't keep company with people who drink. I surround myself with friends and family who understand my past and my temptation and who help guard me against it.

People may get angry if I leave events early or unexpectedly. Some may even think my actions are a bit over the top, but I don't care. I know my past struggles. I'm aware of my weaknesses. I don't indulge in thoughts that may lead me astray or purposely put myself in questionable situations.

Temptations are powerful. So is the Deliverer who helps you to say no. The Holy Spirit will empower you to flee from temptation, should you choose to tap into Him. We have no doubt that He will give you a route of escape.

Take action

Genesis 39 tells the story of Joseph and Potiphar's wife. Potiphar, the captain of the palace guards, had purchased Joseph, a Hebrew slave, from some merchants. God's favor was on Joseph. He prospered in his job as Potiphar's right-hand man. God not only blessed Joseph, but also Potiphar's entire household and property (see Genesis 39:5). Potiphar entrusted this young man with everything and held him in high regard.

Joseph was a good-looking man. This didn't go unnoticed by Potiphar's wife. Day after day she attempted to seduce him, slowly and patiently. And, time after time, Joseph refused her advances.

One day, she actually pulled Joseph toward her physically. "She caught him by his cloak and said, 'Come to bed with me!' But he left his cloak in her hand and ran out of the house" (Genesis 39:12 NIV).

What did Joseph do? He took action. He fled the scene. He ran.

When something comes on television that will ignite your lust, turn it off and walk away.

When someone offers you a drink (*c'mon, just one*), say no and walk away.

When an old flame or new pursuit posts on Facebook, don't respond.

Act quickly and boldly against temptation. Stay strong. Be firm. Don't play around with it. Don't mess with it. Don't even think about it. Flee! Flee! Flee! Run! Run! Run!

Run from sexual sin! No other sin so clearly affects the body as this one does. For sexual immorality is a sin against your own body.

1 Corinthians 6:18 (NLT)

Therefore, my dear friends, flee from idolatry.

1 Corinthians 10:14 (NIV)

Run from anything that stimulates youthful lusts.

2 Timothy 2:22 (NLT)

Another way of taking action is by interrupting the thought. When the devil came a-knocking on Eve's door, she could have shut him down. She could have stopped him in his deceptive rant. She could have interrupted his talk by repeating back what God said.

Interrupt that fantasy.

Interrupt that wonder.

Interrupt that connection.

Interrupt that want.

Interrupt that thought.

Don't entertain certain ideas, dreams, people, or places that may tempt you. Push them out of your mind.

Stay strong in the Word

The Word of God is your handbook for life. When you follow what it says, you align yourself with godly principles. His way of living is not designed to tie you down, withhold fun, or take away your freedom. His directives are to protect you, lead you into His best, shape you into your greatness, and keep you centered in His will.

Revelation 3:10 tells us, "Because you have guarded and kept My word of patient endurance [have held fast the lesson of My patience with the expectant endurance that I give you], I also will keep· you [safe] from the hour of trial [testing] which is coming on the whole world to try those who dwell upon the earth" (AMP).

When you regularly study the Bible, you gain knowledge and truth. You are able to identify the enemy's strategies and tactics. You're prepared. You're ready. You are able to counter temptation with truth, just as Jesus did when He was tempted in the wilderness. And just as Eve should have done in the garden.

I (Darryl) like to say that principles need to come before personalities. Do you think you are too weak-minded to say no to temptation? Are you a social butterfly who often finds yourself in the wrong kind of environment?

Before I surrendered to God, I liked to party. It was a part of my personality. But when I started attaching myself to God's Word, His principles became a part of my lifestyle. It impacted my personality. It influenced my behaviors. It changed my patterns. Today, I run my life by God's standards. I abide in Him, not what my flesh dictates or wants.

Matthew 26:41 tells us to "keep awake (give strict attention, be cautious and active) and watch and pray, that you may not come into temptation. The spirit indeed is willing, but the flesh is weak" (AMP).

When you operate in the flesh, you want more. You are insatiable. Nothing will satisfy. Understand the power of temptation and its domino effect. Saying yes to one wrong thing can lead you down the path of a full-blown affair or relapse.

Choose your way of escape

I like what Nancy Alcorn, the founder of Mercy Ministries, says: "Your way of escape is your choice."

There is always a way out of temptation. You can flee. You can change your number. You can shut down flirtatious advances. You can leave the dinner party. You can leave the shopping mall. You can close down your social media accounts.

Choose not to fall into temptation and you won't. Choose not to participate.

MARRIAGE SAFEGUARDS

The enemy is not going anywhere. Temptations are not going to disappear. You must be aware of the triggers that lead you back into destructive behaviors. And you need to set up safeguards in your marriage to prevent you from stepping into those traps.

We did this, and it was one of the best decisions we ever made as a couple. Here are a few ideas that worked for us.

Safeguard your eyes

As a man, I (Darryl) know a thing or two about roaming eyes. There are attractive women everywhere. It's only human for us to look at something that's easy on the eyes. But, c'mon now! We need to exert some self-discipline.

If you struggle with lust, whether you are a man or woman, you may have to look the other way. Feast your eyes on something else. Don't gape or stare. I know this takes practice. You must work to change it. Be on guard. Recognize when a simple glance turns into deep, lustful desire. It's inappropriate and it's wrong!

Ladies, you are not exempt from visual temptation. A smile, a wink, a kind word from a gorgeous man who desires to draw a little bit closer to you. Or how about a simple glance at a fur coat, pair of shoes, or piece of jewelry that leads to a purchase you can't afford? Or the color of the wine in the glass? Or the new home that you just have to have?

Temptation does not discriminate. It invites itself into everyone's world. It is our job to push it out. Look away.

Safeguard your social life

Where do you go when meeting up with your girlfriends or buddies? Do you frequent the local bar? Where do you go to unwind? A club?

Many men tell me (Darryl), "What's the harm in having a drink with my friends?" If you're doing this in a bar, you're putting yourself in an environment swarming with temptations. A roomful of men and women and flowing alcohol is not the place to safeguard your marriage.

Don't set yourself up for failure. Don't go somewhere that you may be tempted to do the wrong thing. Steer clear of people and places that will ignite a dishonorable desire.

Have a drinking problem? Don't hang out at a bar.

Have a lust problem? Don't go to parties full of beautiful people.

Have a gambling problem? Don't go near a racetrack and stay away from casinos.

Be careful how you spend your social time. Think about what effect, if any, it can have on your marriage and act accordingly. This applies to where you go and with whom.

Whom do you hang out with? Men and women of right influence? Do they sway you to make good decisions? Or do they say things like, "C'mon, loosen up! Have a little fun!" Do they encourage you in your faith or your marriage? Or do they encourage you to complain about your spouse?

Create your social environments with your marriage in mind.

Safeguard your conversations

Watch what you talk about, especially with members of the opposite sex. If you are having a business lunch with someone, leave it at business. Don't get personal. Don't ask what he or she is doing later or delve into intimate conversations. Don't open the door to getting personal.

As a Christian man with my particular past, I know how important it is to be courteous and professional toward women. I'm not a jerk or standoffish, but I watch what I say to them. I don't talk about my marriage, my problems, or other personal things with them. And I don't ask them about theirs.

On a similar note, don't talk badly about your spouse when he or she is not around. This will only hurt your marriage. Watch what you say to them and about them. Engaging in unfit conversation is a way of emotional cheating and breaks down your marriage. Don't do it.

Now how about that little word *gossip*? You meet with your girlfriends for lunch over it. You pick up the phone with the intention to tell all. Untamed tongues run wild when rambling on at another person's expense. Gossip damages reputations and exposes personal faults, sins, circumstances, or defects. Gossip plants seeds of negativity and division. Gossip causes great harm. To people. Marriages (our own and others). Ministries. Our children. Careers.

Life and death are in the power of the tongue. "The tongue can bring death or life; those who love to talk will reap the consequences" (Proverbs 18:21 NLT). Your words have power. Think before you speak. Speak life into the situation, your spouse, your marriage, and others.

Or do not speak at all.

Safeguard social media

A survey from the American Academy of Matrimonial Lawyers indicates that 66 percent of divorce attorneys cite Facebook as the primary source of evidence in divorces. The same survey claims that 20 percent of divorce cases are related to that social media website.

We realize that Facebook is not all bad. It can be a wonderful way to stay connected to family and friends who live far away from us. And many public figures like authors, celebrities, and politicians use it as a platform for their business or message.

We do not use Facebook for personal interests. We have one profile that we share promoting our ministry. We have seen the damage that can come from using this medium for less-than-honorable purposes: Searching for old girlfriends and boyfriends, even ex-wives and ex-husbands. Looking at profiles you wouldn't want your husband to know about. Getting in touch with that friend, which would hurt your wife if she found out.

I (Darryl) always hear people say, "But you just *have* to be on Facebook." No, you don't. What's it for, anyway? How is it really impacting your life? Does writing comments and posting pictures make you a better person?

People are addicted to social media. It's crazy.

Who responded to my comment?

Who likes or dislikes me, my profile pic, or my opinion?

Who is going to feel sorry for me because I blabbed on and on about my horrible life?

Who is going to think highly of me because I blabbed on and on about my wonderful life?

I (Tracy) can't believe how much time, planning, and energy is spent building personal social media profiles and platforms. These people advertise everything about themselves! From what they ate that morning to the dumb thing their husband said to how annoyed they are by midday traffic to what happened at the vet's office with Sparky.

What if each one of us spent all those resources not on Facebook, but on our marriages? What if we started to view our families with the same value we place on social media? What if we checked in with our relationships as much as our personal profiles? What if we signed into our marriages as much as we sign into Facebook? Or Twitter?

I get fired up about this. It is a topic Darryl and I feel strongly about, especially because countless couples who visit us have marriages on the verge of collapse because of sites like Facebook.

Let's turn this around. Let's begin to esteem one another as we should. Let's get our hearts and heads back in the right place. Let's seek God, not the page views of our social media profile.

If you use Facebook for legitimate reasons, great! If not, get rid of your account. If this is too extreme, limit your use. Don't post or look at things you wouldn't want your spouse to see. And don't use Facebook as a sounding board to tell the world how annoying your wife is or how dumb your husband is. Use it in an edifying way.

Safeguard technology and entertainment

Monitor your entertainment. What TV shows do you watch? What movies do you see? What kind of music do you listen to? Engage in entertainment that is uplifting, inspiring, and motivating. And stay away from what causes you to lust.

Here's an experiment. For the next three days, keep track of how you spend your time as it concerns entertainment. Write down what you watch, what you play, and what you listen to. Now ask yourself:

- Is this (TV show, song, video game, movie) causing me to think impure thoughts?

- Is this making me fantasize about someone other than my wife or husband?

■ Is this tempting me to revert back to my old habits (the bad ones)?

If you answer yes, *stop*. Turn it off. Don't watch it. Don't listen to it. Find something else that will build you up instead of tear you down. Do something positive. Read an encouraging book. Go for a walk. Connect with your spouse.

And, yes, you can certainly spend your leisure time watching a movie or sitcom that makes you laugh or is inspiring. We're not suggesting that you only stick to religious entertainment or programming. You don't need to live in a bubble. However, if you struggle in a certain area and a certain movie is going to cause you to stumble, rethink how you unwind.

We also recommend sharing passwords on email accounts and computers. If you have nothing to hide from your spouse, this shouldn't be a problem.

Safeguard your relationship's sore spots

A big temptation comes along whenever you have a disagreement with your spouse. When you feel annoyed, frustrated, or angry with your partner, what's the first thing you want to do? Vent? Down a drink? Take a drive and go somewhere you shouldn't?

Husbands, if you get on the phone or send an email to an old girlfriend or a female acquaintance and start telling her about the fight you just had and what a you-know-what your wife is, chances are that woman is going to say things to make you feel better. She's going to comfort you. And you're going to be more inclined to think this person knows you better or loves you more or is sweeter and nicer than your wife and then . . . wait, there it is . . . a trap. One thing will lead to the next. You hear what I (Darryl) am saying?

The same thing applies to women. If you think your husband is being a jerk and the next minute you're complaining to an old guy friend, you can expect him to be sweet, charming, and try to make you feel better.

When you get into a fight or heated conversation with your spouse and in that moment think, *I just can't stand him/her,* stop.

Pause.

Think.

Don't do anything drastic.

Don't do anything you wouldn't do had that argument never happened.

Don't run off and get loaded.

Don't storm off and hang out with friends who are a negative influence.

Don't hide out and do something secretive.

If I'm on the road and Tracy and I get into a fight on the phone, I don't run off to the nearest nightclub or say yes to that party full of women, just because we are experiencing tension. My way of living stays the same. I don't change my programming. I focus on something else. I work out. Or take a walk. Or pray. I wait for the emotions to pass. I deal with it properly.

When you are feeling overly emotional, you have a better chance of acting out. Don't. Do the same thing you would do with a level head and with God in mind.

WARNING: YOU ARE MOST VULNERABLE
AFTER SPIRITUAL VICTORIES

Ever experience a personal revival and make a commitment to God to change? You know, like when you hear the pastor preaching at church and you begin to feel uncomfortable about your occasional dabbling in pornography. Or you come back from a marriage retreat with a strong desire to be less selfish and keep your husband's interests above yours. Or God speaks to your heart during your quiet time and you promise to prioritize Him in your life.

What usually happens following these emotionally and spiritually charged events?

Temptation shows up.

The devil uses those moments to ambush you and derail your intentions. Notice how a cute coworker starts flirting with you. Or a friend invites you to an after-hours party. Or you see a fabulous watch or pair of shoes that you just have to have—and can't afford.

Spiritual victories are often followed by testing.

Immediately after Jesus was baptized and the Spirit of God descended on Him, Jesus went into the wilderness on a forty-day fast. There the devil tempted Him physically, spiritually, and regarding his purpose on earth.

On three separate occasions the enemy tried to get Jesus to fall by offering Him material pleasures, power, even the world. The devil twisted the words of God, hoping that Jesus would begin to doubt. It's interesting that this happened right after a time of spiritual renewal.

The devil came and said to him [Jesus], "If you are the Son of God, tell these stones to become loaves of bread."

Matthew 4:3 (NLT)

Notice the enemy tempted Jesus with what He needed and desired the most in his current condition—food. The devil will tempt you in the same way.

What is it that your flesh desires? Are you lonely and desire companionship? Do you feel unfulfilled and seek satisfaction? Are you a workaholic who chases every idea or venture that promises to bring riches and power? When tough times come are you tempted to lay down your faith in search of false peace?

How is the devil trying to get you to walk away from God and your marriage? Do you think life is better somewhere else? Do you want a more beautiful, thinner, younger wife? A husband with more energy and money to lavish on you? A carefree life without the responsibility of family?

Jesus doesn't budge and tells the devil, "No! The Scriptures say, 'People do not live by bread alone, but by every word that comes from the mouth of God'" (Matthew 4:4 NLT).

The cycle of the enemy's temptations and Jesus's refusal to fall for the trap happened two more times. (Read Matthew 4 to get the full story.) Jesus passed each test with flying colors because He relied on and trusted in God. Then He was ready for promotion, to walk in His purpose and begin his public ministry.

Think about what may await you after passing the test of temptation. Think of the possibilities. Your breakthrough may manifest when you finally say *no*. Your marriage may be restored after you stand firm in Christ. Your spouse may recommit his or her life to God after you stay in obedience.

Don't lose heart. Don't lose hope. Keep the faith. Keep trusting in God.

THINK OF THE RIGHT THINGS

When in doubt, keep your mind on good things, the right things. Sometimes we get so focused on what *not* to do that we forget what we should do.

> *And, now, dear brothers and sisters, one final thing. Fix your thoughts on what is true, and honorable, and right, and pure, and lovely, and admirable. Think about things that are excellent and worthy of praise.*
>
> Philippians 4:8 (NLT)

Think of what an awesome father your husband is.
Think of all the sacrifices your wife makes.
Think of your beautiful children.
Think of grace.
Think of how much God loves you.
Think of how you fell in love with your spouse.
Speak goodness into your life, your marriage, and your spouse as if it is already happening.

If your marriage is in shambles or you can't think of anything good about it or your spouse, think good things anyway. Build your faith and speak life into what feels dead. Think of reconnecting instead of isolating. Think of becoming more emotionally in tune. Think of the rekindling of passion.

Seek God and His work in your marriage. "Blessed (happy, to

be envied) is the man who is patient under trial and stands up under temptation, for when he has stood the test and been approved, he will receive [the victor's] crown of life which God has promised to those who love Him" (James 1:12 AMP).

Be aware of temptation and know that there is a way out. Guard your gates. Interrupt the temptation. Choose the way of escape.

SOMETHING TO THINK ABOUT

Temptations are real. And very powerful.

You may have already experienced the pain and heartache of falling into temptation. Or you may have been on the receiving side and felt the devastating residual effects of broken trust and deep, personal betrayal.

Perhaps the opposite sex is not a temptation for you, but you are weak in other areas. Maybe you have a nagging addiction. A desire to be recognized that you try to fulfill by gaining emotional attention from someone other than your spouse. An eating disorder that consumes your entire life. A spending problem that has depleted your bank account.

What are the possible sources of temptation for you? What will happen if you choose not to say no and fall into the deadly trap?

Think about some ways you can begin to safeguard these areas. Perhaps you can attend a support group or find a mentor who will help keep you accountable. Plan in advance what you will do the next time temptation stares at you. Will you call your spouse for help? Leave the party? Cut up your credit cards?

Having an escape plan already decided will make your exit that much easier.

Remember, God has already provided you a way out of whatever tempts you. All you have to do is choose your escape. You can be victorious. You can say no. With the power of the Holy Spirit, you can resist what your flesh desires and what the enemy wants to use to destroy you and your marriage.

10

A New Beginning

As we enter the final chapter in this book, know that this is not the end. It's only the beginning.

It is our hope and confidence that you have embarked on the beginning of a new journey, a great adventure, a call to experience God's best in your life and in your marriage.

Maybe you started reading this book with a mix of skepticism and desperate hope. Maybe you were doubtful anything could change. Perhaps you were even toying with the word *divorce.*

Are you hopeful that your marriage can be transformed?

Are you confident that God can restore what you or your spouse may have broken?

Are you excited by some of the changes you have seen in yourself?

Are you looking forward to the rest of your marriage with optimism?

Has your faith increased?

Has your mind been renewed?

Has your spirit been recharged?

We are thinking about you as we close this book. We are praying that the words that we have been inspired by God to write have already begun a new work in your heart—a work that is moving through and changing you and ultimately your marriage.

Take a walk with us from the beginning. Let's revisit what we've talked about and what you've learned. As time passes, use this chapter as a refresher repeatedly and frequently as you embark on the healing chapter.

You may have found common ground with us as we entered into marriage with absolute brokenness. Can you relate to how desperately we needed God not only to heal our marriage but also to restore our individual hearts?

We didn't trust ourselves or each other when we got married. We dived into saying "I do" with suspicion. One eye always open, protecting our hearts. Hurt people hurt people. We hurt each other through our defensiveness, through fighting dirty, through ignoring each other, through purposely pushing each other's hot buttons, through throwing past mistakes in the other's face, through our selfishness.

Then, we surrendered. First to God, then to ourselves. And through His transforming power and the challenging process of change, we found ourselves and we found each other.

Have you opened your heart, your past, your failures, your disappointments, your letdowns, and your fears and handed them over to God? Maybe you've done this willingly. Maybe you've kicked and screamed against it the entire way.

God loves you so much. He loves you with all His heart. He pursues you in your messes and even in your disobedience. His greatest desire is to empower you with His love so that you are equipped to go out and love one another.

The Bible says that those who truly love God, obey Him (John 14:21, 24). Those who know Him hear His voice and follow Him (John 10:17). Those who abide in Him and His Word know the truth (John 14:17; 17:17).

And then what happens?

Something amazing!

The truth sets us free!

Have you experienced this freedom?

Have you felt a relief, a peace that cannot be explained?

Have you recommitted your faith, your marriage, into God's hands, trusting His divine love to heal your hurts?

If you pursue God and His ways, you will find salvation for your soul and the resurrecting power you desire within your marriage. He will make all things new.

A GOD'S-EYE VIEW OF MARRIAGE

A renewed marriage takes a little (okay, a lot) more than church attendance and a shout of praise. It begins with the proper definition and expectations about marriage. God clearly defines that truth in His Word.

What God says about marriage may have rocked your world. He designed the marriage relationship to develop a man and a wife into His image. To mature you into love, joy, peace, patience, kindness, goodness, faithfulness, gentleness, and self-control. These characteristics make you capable of love and of emulating the person of Jesus Christ.

Marriage is not about finding your soul mate or relying on another person to meet your needs and fulfill you as an individual. You do not marry to change your spouse or to fill in the holes, or mend the brokenness in your soul and spirit.

It's about giving, serving your spouse as Christ serves the church. It's about living according to God's ways, not what the magazines, books, or people on TV say. It's about helping one another get to heaven.

Marriage is so much greater than you! It enables you to impact this world for Him.

THE IMPORTANCE OF
PERSONAL HEALING

Before you can begin the work of change in your marriage, you need to turn the focus on yourself. You must become vulnerable. Honest. Open. You must travel with God into the deep places in your heart where the real issues lie.

You must dig down to the source of your defensiveness. Or fear of the future. Or anger at the world. Or bitterness. Or doubt. And you must allow God to perform spiritual surgery and remedy your internal sickness.

Yes, it may mean reopening old wounds. Entering into emotional territory you had hoped never to visit again. Maybe you finally will deal with the man who abused you when you were a little girl. Or admit to painful mistakes you made that caused a downward spiral of bad decisions and lifetime consequences. Or come face-to-face with that family member who betrayed you. Or finally tell the truth about your addiction.

Have you felt challenged by this process? Have you been afraid to explore some of these areas? Are you holding back? Or have you run into the arms of God and leaned into His perfect restoration process?

THE REMEDY OF FORGIVENESS

Forgiveness plays a big part in moving forward in your life and in your marriage. We know this is a subject of deep struggle.

Has your wife's betrayal caused you so much pain that you can't stomach lying beside her in bed? Have your husband's infidelities blinded you to the possibility of reconciliation? Do the words *I forgive you* leave a bad taste in your mouth?

Unforgiveness is the enemy's way of holding you hostage to bitterness and anger. It poisons your soul and torments your mind. You may feel it's impossible to receive or achieve.

Be encouraged. Jesus has already accomplished forgiveness for you. Through His death and resurrection, He has made you more than a conqueror. You are victorious. You can overcome. There is no situation, no circumstance, no person, no devil in hell, no affair, no addiction, no betrayal, and no lie that can hold you back.

Can you see it? The light at the end of the tunnel? A glimpse of hope?

You are free to forgive. God will give you the power and do a mighty work in you if you get on board with Him, trust Him, and surrender to forgiveness.

Release!
Give up that grudge.
Get rid of bitterness.
Bid resentment good-bye.
Forgive. Today. Right now.

LIVING IN A ONE-SIDED MARRIAGE

Has your spouse checked out? Is your wife deep in an addiction that stops her from being present in your marriage? Is your husband still having an affair with that woman?

When you are a spouse-in-waiting, you feel like you are living in defeat. You may want to make things work in your marriage, but you can't because one spouse isn't living right. Unless both partners are doing the right thing, the bond will remain broken.

We know. This is very discouraging. If you're in this situation, you may want to check out, too. But unless God has released you from the marriage according to His Word, you must learn how to rise up and rise above the brokenness. Build while believing and use your power of choice!

Do not just survive each day. Learn to thrive. Choose to live well and be well. Whole. Healthy. And with joy.

When your spouse has not stopped the cycle of sin, turn to God. Make a decision to let Him lead you through this process. We know it's not easy to trust when you don't know what will happen with your marriage in the future. The unknown can be scary. But that's the point of trusting. That's why we need faith. Believe, even against what may seem impossible, that God can breathe life into you and your marriage.

There are also certain practical steps that you need to take to protect yourself in your marriage, whether it's protecting your heart or protecting your household. If you have a codependent relationship with your husband or wife, sever the ties. Not with him or her but with the behavior. Stop cleaning up, covering up, and correcting your spouse's messes.

Remember the powerful principle of building while believing. Just because your spouse is not on board in your marriage doesn't mean you should lie down and play dead. Activate your faith. Cultivate friendships with those who are faith minded and positive. Get involved in your community. Volunteer. Serve in the church. Get a job. Start a career. Get going.

Protect your household and plan for your future. And set some boundaries. Assure your spouse of your love, but explain that until he or she stops the drugs, the drinking, the gambling, the shopping, the addiction, or the affair, you will withhold your trust.

REBUILDING TRUST

When you work to reconnect with your spouse after a betrayal, you commit to rebuilding broken trust. It's not an easy process, but it is possible. And very rewarding.

Are you in the position where you need to prove yourself "trustworthy"? Do the right thing. Over and over. Again and again. Day in and day out.

Do the right thing even if your feelings tell you otherwise.

Do the right thing even when you're tired.

Do the right thing even (and especially) when nobody is looking.

Do the right thing, not to guarantee a certain outcome, but to obey God.

Has your husband or wife broken your trust? Set up boundaries to protect your heart, but stay engaged in the rebuilding process. What are some things you can ask for that will help ease your mind as you work together? Don't abuse this component of rebuilding to punish your spouse. And don't constantly rehash the offense.

Rebuilding trust takes time and patience. Be mindful and sensitive to each other's feelings and needs. Change your perspective and begin to celebrate the daily victories. This takes the pressure off the bigger picture of reconciliation. Keep it simple but make it real. You are worth the gift that is waiting for you on the other side.

Forgiveness

Freedom

Restoration

A new start!

BE MINDFUL AT ALL TIMES

Selfishness is the root of most divorces. It's easy to be me-me-me minded, but in God's design, marriage is about being spouse minded.

It's about being mindful.

When you stop paying attention to your marriage and your spouse and live with the notion that everything is about you, your marriage suffers. Your relationship with your husband or wife suffers. Everyone suffers.

Pay attention. At all times.

How well do you know your spouse? Not just his or her likes and dislikes. Take it a step further. What is going on in your wife's heart? In your husband's thoughts? What is your spouse's love language?

Take the time to reconnect with your partner. This might mean saying no to less important things like hanging out with your buddy or going shopping with a friend. Get to know them. This is how you live in love.

What is happening in your marriage? What is happening to your spouse? Is he or she lonely? Neglected? Trying to do everything on his or her own? Feeling overwhelmed by the stress of work?

Pay attention to every aspect of your marriage. Feelings. Finances. Sex life. Ruts. Responsibilities. How you treat one another.

What is your communication like? Do you talk more than you listen? Do you listen to only what you want to hear? Are you prone to shutting down? Watch what you say and how you say it. Choose your words wisely. And don't fight dirty. Don't engage in language that you know will hurt your husband or wife.

Show up in your marriage. Stop living outside your relationship and busying yourself with other things. Spend time with your wife. Spend time with your husband. Spend time with your children.

When you are mindful of your marriage and your spouse, things change. You change. You become aware of what's important, what needs to be dealt with, what needs to be restored.

GOD'S BLUEPRINT FOR MARRIAGE

You know by now that God's ways are the best ways. That includes His plans for marriage as recorded in His Word.

Were you encouraged to learn there is a divine plan for marriage?

Were you challenged by His blueprint?

Did it revolutionize your thinking?

First and foremost, a marriage must be grounded in faith. God is number one. You need to live as an individual and as a spouse with God as your center.

Second, God doesn't want us to be lonely. That is why He gives us a helpmate. You and your spouse are in this thing called *life* together. You work together as a team during good times and bad times.

Third, as husband and wife you are called to specific roles. Men, spiritually guide your family. Take your rightful place as the head of your household, not as a dictator or sadistic ruler but as a loving, understanding, and honoring husband and father.

Women, submit to your husband. Respect him. Give him the space and position to lead your family in God's ways. Show him your love by honoring him with your words and with your actions.

Partner together to serve God as Christ serves the church.

Fourth, enjoy sex with your spouse. Yes, that's right! Have fun. Don't use it to manipulate the other or withhold because you're angry. Use this intimate experience to draw closer together. God created the marriage bed. It's part of being married!

Fifth, steward your money wisely. This means creating and sticking with a budget, stopping foolish spending, and making smart purchases. Most of all, it means honoring God with the money He has given you. He is your source, after all. Not your job, not your boss, not the economy, not the stock market. Tithes give Him what is rightfully His. God will bless you and your family for your obedience.

Sixth, raise godly children. Be the example you want them to follow. Make God a priority. Don't just tell them faith is important. Show them through your actions.

BEWARE OF TEMPTATION

We don't care how Christian you think you are. How much you read your Bible. How many church services you attend. How many books about faith you read. You are not immune to temptation. It's out there. And the enemy is just waiting for you to fall into its trap.

The key to winning the war against temptation is to be aware of your vulnerability and to abide in God. Without Him, it's easy to become quickly ensnared by the opposite sex, by drugs, by alcohol, by food, by an addiction, or by anything that can take your eyes off God.

Another key is to set up safeguards. What do you need to do to protect yourself and your marriage?

Do you have to limit your use of Facebook and other social media accounts?

Do you have to share passwords?

Do you have to stop hanging out with certain friends?

Do you have to nix boys' night out at the bar?

Do you have to leave a party where everyone is drinking?

Do you have to stop having lunch with your assistant?

Do you have to stop having dinner with your coworker?

Find your escape when faced with temptation. Run. Take action. Say no. Look the other way.

DARRYL'S PARTING THOUGHTS

The greatest gift Tracy and I have ever received was God calling us into full-time ministry. There are so many people in the church who are broken, who are not free. And there are so many marriages that are torn apart, husbands and wives who are ready to give up and throw in the towel.

We stand before you knowing what that looks like, what it feels like. And we also stand before you knowing what it's like for God to break through a mess. I can't imagine what our lives would look like today had we not allowed Him to come through for us. Surely our marriage would have crumbled. God's ministry through us would not exist. This book would never have been written. And most of all, God's salvation, power, glory, and love through us would not be revealed.

God's wholeness awaits not just you, but your spouse, too! If you feel as though you are in this marriage alone, you're not. God can work miracles. He's in the business of transformation and restoration. He can deliver you and your spouse from whatever is holding you back from living the marriage He has designed for you. A marriage of wholeness, wellness, vitality, love, and, yes, even passion.

Friend, if you're on the verge of quitting, you haven't even tapped into the amazing part of your marriage and what God has in store for you and your family.

If you let Him, God will blow your mind. Let Him run your life. Let Him lead your marriage. Participate in the healing process and watch Him do miraculous things.

> *[Earnestly] remember the former things, [which I did] of old; for I am God, and there is no one else; I am God, and there is none like Me, Declaring the end and the result from the beginning, and from ancient times the things that are not yet done, saying, My counsel shall stand, and I will do all My pleasure and purpose. . . . Yes, I have spoken, and I will bring it to pass; I have purposed it, and I will do it.*
>
> *Isaiah 46:9–11 (AMP)*

Men, want to see a change in your life and your marriage? Find your identity in Christ. God will teach you how to be a real man. He will show you how to treat your wife. He will empower you through His Word, not worldly principles. Take the time to get to know Him, to surrender to His transformation. The world will set you up for failure, but God will set you up for life.

I think about what Tracy and I have overcome and my heart is amazed. Our relationship is strong today only because we understand God's truth and we live by what He says. No, we don't have a perfect marriage. But we didn't give up.

Keep trying. Don't give up. Continue to pick yourselves up and move forward. Trust God, not your feelings. You may not like your wife right now. You may want to run away from your marriage. You may be tempted to look for a sexual thrill elsewhere. You may feel like the process of change isn't worth it. You may feel discouraged. You may feel tired.

Even when your feelings are valid, you cannot let them over-rule what is right. You cannot let them talk you into doing what is wrong or checking out. A real Christian is a Christ follower. You give up your old way of living, die to self, and rise again into the life and ways of Jesus. Dying to self means dying to the pursuit of sinful pleasures, desires and selfishness. You are no longer living for yourself, but for God. Marriages fall apart because the two people within the marriage will not die to self. That is the deep and the whole truth. Feelings can be dangerous. Don't rely on them.

God says life is about faith, not feelings. "For we live by faith, not by sight" (2 Corinthians 5:7 NIV). Don't make decisions and take action based on feelings in your current situation. Live in Him regardless of what is happening around you, regardless of how your marriage looks, and regardless of how you feel about it.

Keep doing the right thing.

Keep loving your wife.

Keep saying no to temptation.

Keep God in the center of your life.

Keep working on yourself.

Keep forgiving.

Keep rebuilding trust.

Keep showing up.

Keep being mindful of your spouse.

Keep believing that "God, who began the good work within you, will continue his work until it is finally finished" (Philippians 1:6 NLT).

Let us not become weary in doing good,
for at the proper time we will reap a harvest if we do not
give up.

Galatians 6:9 *(NIV)*

A NOTE FROM TRACY

There is a reason that half of America's population is divorced today, many multiple times, and why our ministry email is full of hurting, defeated people living in marriages that are painful, empty, and unproductive.

People are not doing life or marriage the way that God had in mind. Many don't even know how.

I hope that this book has shed some light on some fundamentals necessary to sustain a whole, healthy marriage. There is a great need to get down deep into some basic daily applications. You can read all the Scripture verses you'd like, but until you make the decision to die to yourself, put that Word to work, become a true follower of Christ, live according to God's standards, and mindfully love one another, nothing will change. We as a people must change.

My precious friend, God has not forgotten about you. He's waiting for you. His freedom awaits you! Let's come together and fix this problem. Let's rise up and stop the hurt, sorrow, and destruction. Marriage was never designed to be like this. Be hopeful. You can experience it the way God designed it to be.

You and your spouse are worthy of a new start. And God wants to give it to you. He wants you to experience a new relationship that is better than anything you've ever known. You can die to that old marriage and be raised up into a new one.

Live what you have learned.

Bury the past.

Embrace the process.

Follow Christ and surrender to the Holy Spirit.

He makes all things new!

This means that anyone who belongs to Christ has become a new person.
The old life is gone; a new life has begun!

2 *Corinthians 5:17 (NLT)*